Condition Of The Border At The Union

You are holding a reproduction of an original work that is in the public domain in the United States of America, and possibly other countries. You may freely copy and distribute this work as no entity (individual or corporate) has a copyright on the body of the work. This book may contain prior copyright references, and library stamps (as most of these works were scanned from library copies). These have been scanned and retained as part of the historical artifact.

This book may have occasional imperfections such as missing or blurred pages, poor pictures, errant marks, etc. that were either part of the original artifact, or were introduced by the scanning process. We believe this work is culturally important, and despite the imperfections, have elected to bring it back into print as part of our continuing commitment to the preservation of printed works worldwide. We appreciate your understanding of the imperfections in the preservation process, and hope you enjoy this valuable book.

THE RESEARCH LIBRARY

Condition of the Border
at the Union

Uniform in Style with this Volume

THE COMMERCIAL RELATIONS

OF

ENGLAND AND PORTUGAL

OTHERS TO FOLLOW

GILNOCKIE TOWER AND HOLLOWS BRIDGE

1907

Condition of the Border at the Union

Destruction of the Graham Clan

By
John Graham

SECOND EDITION

LONDON
GEORGE ROUTLEDGE & SONS, Limited
New York: E. P. DUTTON & CO.
1907

DA
880
.B72
G74
1907

THIS WORK
IS DEDICATED, BY KIND PERMISSION,
TO
THE RIGHT HONOURABLE LORD MUNCASTER,
LORD-LIEUTENANT OF CUMBERLAND

PREFACE

MUCH light has recently been thrown upon a peculiarly interesting period of Border history by the diligent researches of Sir Maxwell Lyte and his colleagues of the National Manuscripts Commission.

Although we have abundant records of all the great Border events of the sixteenth century down to the death of Elizabeth, it is surprising how little we accurately know of the barbarous methods employed in the final overthrow of the Border clans at the time of the Union of the two Kingdoms, when James Stuart of Scotland mounted the throne as James the First of Great Britain.

And yet there was nothing in the history of that memorable reign (save perhaps the gunpowder plot) of greater political importance, and surely there was nothing of greater dramatic interest.

Curiously, neither Hume nor Lingard give so much as a single page to the discussion of this great question which stood supremely first among the problems calling for solution, by reason of the great change in the government of the two kingdoms. One might almost be inclined to think there had been a conspiracy of silence, arising from a sense of shame, regarding the dark details of Court intrigue, confiscations, banishments, and indiscriminate executions in the Border towns, which stained the opening years of the United Kingdom.

The largest clan in number, at this period, though of small importance as a fighting force, was that of the Grahams of Eskdale. Their lands were the most valuable and extensive on the Border, and the natural fertility of the soil had begun to lure the community, in continually increasing numbers, into the peaceful pursuits of tillage. Still a large number of the clan were avowed raiders, as their fathers had been, but neither better nor worse than their neighbours of other clans on both sides of the Border. And the only apparent reason why immediate and merciless destruction fell upon the Grahams on the accession of King James, was their possession of those valuable acres which the King had been persuaded to confer, as a free gift, upon one of his worthless favourites, who chanced to be a personage of importance in the north country.

Among the descendants of the Eskdale clan there are stories in circulation to this day of the calamities which overwhelmed the homes of their forefathers in the days of King James, but these woeful tales of ancient date, with little or no historical corroboration, had for the most part faded away into the category of myths. Even the Border ballad writers, to whom we are so much indebted for our knowledge of the deeds of other days, are silent regarding the enormities of the Eskdale crusade.

We are therefore greatly indebted to the indefatigable industry of the National Manuscripts Commission in bringing to light from the archives of various historical mansions on the Border, papers and letters, giving so much interesting—indeed, in some cases, almost sensational confirmation, of much that had come to be considered as old wives' stories, or little more than historical cobwebs.

The most valuable collection of these ancient papers is that belonging to Lord Muncaster, at Muncaster Castle.

They are kept in large iron boxes in the Muniment Room (a curious vaulted chamber constructed in the thickness of the wall, in this fine old border mansion), and in these documents we have a fairly perfect record of the extraordinary proceedings at Carlisle, where King James' Commission met, ostensibly for the general pacification of the Border, but really for a very different purpose.

Thinking it might be interesting to many of my Border friends, especially those of my own race, I have made a selection from those papers of certain of the most remarkable facts which I shall endeavour to string into narrative as clearly as one unpractised in the art of literary exposition may hope to succeed in doing. At the outset, however, I find the task I have set myself involves a good deal more labour and research than I anticipated, as no clear understanding of the evil conditions existing on the Border at the time of the Union is possible without a preliminary glance at the extraordinary current of political events which gave birth to, and gradually developed, the system of raiding or rieving.

How the Moss-trooper grew into power and importance as a defender of his country's frontier, and why he was allowed to attain to fighting capabilities so dangerous and difficult to control, has been so exhaustively dealt with by Mr Bruce Armstrong in his *History of Liddesdale*, and by the Rev. Robert Borland in his *Border Raids and Raiders*, that I would recommend the perusal of these excellent works to all who are keenly interested in Border lore. It will, however, be necessary in this little book to glance at several of those critical events of the sixteenth century which engendered the fierce international hatred, mainly instrumental in creating that unprecedented compound of humanity in which were mingled so many of the qualities we most admire, with others which we most abhor, known to history as the warrior, patriot, and freebooter of the Border. Some of those events, apart from their historical importance, possess a fascinating air of romance peculiarly their own. They exhibit so many instances of bravery, fidelity, and deeds of humanity even amidst the uproar and slaughter of the fray that to this day over the Border land, if anywhere, the spirit of chivalry has a traditional right to brood.

J. G.

HUNTINGSTILE, GRASMERE

CONTENTS

	PAGE
PREFACE	vii

CHAPTER I
ORIGIN OF THE RAIDER

Invasions of Edward — Sack of Berwick — Scott of Buccleuch—Methods of the Raider - - - 1

CHAPTER II
PRIMITIVE COURTS OF JUSTICE

Punitive Expeditions under the Earl of Angus—Blackmail — Warden's Court — Abuse of power by the Warden—Formalities of the Court—Deadly Feuds—Beacon Lights—Debateable Land - - 9

CHAPTER III
LORD MAXWELL

Invasion of Debateable Land by Lord Dacre—Defeated by the Armstrongs — Armstrongs excluded from Carlisle Market—Reprisals—Helplessness of Lord Dacre—Bothwell Keeper of Liddesdale—Unruly Barons of the West Marches—Advance of James V. towards the Border — Execution of Cockburn of Henderland - - - - - - 22

CHAPTER IV

JOHNIE ARMSTRONG

Lord Maxwell and Charteris of Amisfield experts in cattle-lifting—Disobedience of the Border Barons—Maxwell's jealousy of Gilnockie—King James at Carlinrigg—Murder of Gilnockie - - - 32

CHAPTER V

WRATH OF KING HENRY VIII

Loyalty of the Armstrongs shaken—Raids into Northumberland—Anger of the English King—Invasion of Scotland under the Earl of Hertford—Second invasion under Euer—Battle of Ancrum Moor - 42

CHAPTER VI

THE SEVENTH EARL OF NORTHUMBERLAND

Northumberland Warden of Eastern and Middle Marches—His great popularity on the Border—Hostility of Cecil—Catholic rising—Northumberland involved—Takes refuge in Liddesdale—Heroism of his devoted Wife - - - - - - - 48

CHAPTER VII

NORTHUMBERLAND BETRAYED

Treachery of Hector Armstrong of Harelaw—Northumberland captured—A Prisoner in Loch Leven Castle—Sold to England by the Scottish Regent for ten thousand crowns - - - - - 66

CHAPTER VIII

THE COUNTESS BETRAYED

Heroic efforts of the Countess to save her husband's life
—Northumberland landed at Dunbar and executed
at York—Widespread indignation at his death   -   77

CHAPTER IX

EXTENSIVE RIEVING

Great claims for plunder on both sides of the Border—
The Grahams accused as chief offenders   -   -   86

CHAPTER X

BUCCLEUCH AND KINMONT WILLIE

Rescue of Kinmont from Carlisle Castle—Angry correspondence between Elizabeth and James—Lord Scrope invades Liddesdale—Barbarous treatment of Women and Children   -   -   -   -   92

CHAPTER XI

EMBARRASSMENT OF KING JAMES

Buccleuch imprisoned in Blackness Castle—Surrenders to Queen Elizabeth—Carey's terror of his Prisoner—Buccleuch pardoned—His memorable reception by Queen Elizabeth   -   -   -   -   -   100

CHAPTER XII

ACCESSION OF KING JAMES

The Grahams—Their Settlement in Cumberland—Union of the Kingdoms—Enthusiastic Reception of King James in England—His extraordinary Vanity—Belief in his own Wisdom—Belief in Witchcraft—The impecunious Scottish Nobility—Bestowal of Titles and Rewards - - - - - 105

CHAPTER XIII

THE KING'S PASSION FOR FAVOURITES

His Desire for complete Incorporation opposed in both Countries—The Favourites Somerset and Buckingham—Plain Speaking on the Part of Foreign Ambassadors - - - - 117

CHAPTER XIV

THE EARL OF CUMBERLAND

Lord Cumberland English Warden of the Western Marches—His Favour with the King—Denunciation of the Grahams—Moral and Social Condition of the Cumbrian Gentry in 1605—Odious Criminals sheltered by the Authorities—Disturbances of the 'Ill Week'—The Lands of the Grahams confiscated and conferred as a Free Grant upon Lord Cumberland - - - - - - 125

CHAPTER XV

COMMISSION APPOINTED

Commissioners for the Pacification of the Border—All local Men selected—Sir Wilfred Lawson—One hundred and forty-nine Grahams summoned an

imprisoned in Carlisle Castle — Transported to
Holland — Charges against Hutchin Graham —
Efforts in Favour of the Grahams—Hollows and
Netherby garrisoned—Division of Opinion between
Scottish and English Commissioners   -   -   133

CHAPTER XVI

PROGRESS OF THE CRUSADE

Petition of the banished Grahams—Their Escape from
Holland—Twenty-four of them rejoin their Families
in Eskdale—Resentment of King James—Indiscriminate Executions—Sir William Cranston's unwillingness to act against the Grahams — His
excellent Services on the Border — Cumbrian
Criminals employed as Agents by Lord Cumberland—Increasing Hostility between Scottish and
English Commissioners regarding Malefactors   - 146

CHAPTER XVII

BORDERERS SUSPECTED OF TREASON

The Gunpowder Plot—Lord Northumberland and Sir
Wilfred Lawson in Danger—Rigour of the Penal
Laws against Catholics—Alarm of Sir Wilfred
Lawson—His Protestations of Loyalty accepted—
Northumberland condemned   -   -   -   157

CHAPTER XVIII

THE BISHOP OF CARLISLE

The Bishop of Carlisle added to the Commission—Death
of Lord Cumberland — Absurd Claims of his
Successor—Captain of Bewcastle secretly aids the
Armstrongs in their Raids—Great Severities in
Eskdale—Signs of public Resentment—King re-
proves the Commissioners for their Cruelty—

Curious Petition from Walter Graham of Netherby
—Proceedings against Hutchin Graham for the
rescue of Kinmont Willie—Murder of Barngleese
for Plunder by John Musgrave—He is excused
by the Bishop of Carlisle - - - - 164

CHAPTER XIX

THE BOGS OF ROSCOMMON

Continued Persecutions in Eskdale—Appointment of
Lord Dunbar—Frequency of Capital Punishment—
Banishment of the Grahams to Ireland—Sir Ralph
Sadler—Starvation in the Bogs of Roscommon - 179

CHAPTER XX

FINAL PACIFICATION OF THE BORDER

Return of the Grahams from Ireland—Embarrassment of
the Government—Arrival of Buccleuch from the
Belgic Wars—He is entrusted with ample Powers
for the Pacification of the Border - - - 193

CONDITION OF THE BORDER

CHAPTER I

ORIGIN OF THE RAIDER

THE position which the native of the Borderland occupied was, probably, unique in history. It was his destiny to be a dweller on that extremely short land frontier between two ever-hostile kingdoms. His family, his home, and all his belongings were ever within the zone of military operations, where there was little respite from the clash of arms, and where his good sword was the only guarantee for his life and his property.

In the long but unsuccessful struggles during the time of the Edwards—notably Edward I, called the Hammer of Scotland—to reduce the Scots to a state of vassalage, the Borderland was sorely smitten, for there fell the first shock of the English invasion, reducing the inhabitants at times to ruin and misery. Frequently, without the least warning, the invader broke in and swept the land like a tempest; whole families were massacred, and their lands laid waste, as if by a bolt from the blue. In those days news travelled slowly. There were none of those preliminary warnings by electric agency of strained relations or ultimatums to which we are accustomed in modern times. Fearful as were those invasions, however, they never succeeded in completely crushing the irregular border warrior, who, for so many long years, checked their progress northward.

Every blow from England was returned with interest, and there were times when both sides of the Border lay in ashes for miles north and south. The English invader had not only to reckon with men of dauntless valour and great powers of endurance, but with men whose recuperative powers and cunning tricks of ambush made them equally dangerous and perplexing. The heaviest reverses might scatter and reduce, but could never quite crush the Border clansmen. Defeat only drove them back to the shelter of their hinterlands among the ravines of Tarras or the upper reaches of Liddesdale, there to gather up their strength, to repair their losses, and to mature their plans of retaliation upon the foe.

At times when the enemy, feeling confident of his conquest, would be tempted to relax his vigilance on the march, he would find himself suddenly ambushed. A wild torrent of Armstrongs and Elliots, whom he had apparently just defeated, would swoop down upon him like a hurricane, driving his dismayed and broken forces far beyond the Esk or the Eden.

Again and again the assaults of England were checked and repulsed by the clansmen of the Border, whose loyalty and patriotism, in defending their native land, were altogether forgotten when, in after years, their descendants were so cruelly crushed when their services were no longer needed.

We must go a long way back for the origin of that deadly hatred which existed between the two countries for ages. It probably had its root in the savage invasions of Edward in the earlier years of the fourteenth century in his rude attempt to conquer Scotland. Had a friendly union of the two kingdoms been possible in those early days, all the political conditions of Europe might have been modified thereby. The splendid energies of the British race would not have been crushed and neutralised by internal disorders. The British Isles would have been able to offer united action against foreign enemies, and, as the kingdom would have been saved from ages of feuds and bloodshed, it is likely that the Border raider would never have been called into existence.

The savage policy of Edward, however, rendered union impossible, as he made no attempt to gain the goodwill of the Scots, but rather treated them as vermin fit only for slavery or extermination. In pursuance of his barbarous policy he fell upon the Border without provocation and without warning, capturing Berwick under circumstances of such atrocity as could never be forgotten, and which laid the foundation for centuries of international ill-will. The destruction of this chief Border town is described by Tytler as follows:

'All the horrors of a rich and populous city, sacked by an inflamed soldiery and a commander thirsting for vengeance now succeeded. Seventeen thousand persons, without distinction of age or sex, were put to the sword, and for two days the city ran with blood like a river. The churches, to which the miserable inhabitants fled for sanctuary, were violated and defiled with blood, spoiled of their ornaments, and turned into stables for English cavalry.'

Little wonder that Scotland was staggered at this wholesale butchery of the inhabitants of her most important mercantile city, whose only crime was their refusal to open their gates on the imperious summons of the invader; and still less wonder that, from this fatal day arose that unquenchable hatred which blazed between England and Scotland through so many generations. On the fall of Berwick a cry for vengeance rang throughout the land, uniting all the Border tribes for the invasion of England. An army of considerable force was organised, and under the command of the Earls of Ross, Monteith, and Atholl overran Northumberland. Redesdale and Tyndale were laid waste; the monasteries of Lanercost and Hexham were given to the flames, and the country, far and wide, swept of all its cattle and movables.

Edward retaliated by advancing against Dunbar with an army so large that any resistance the Scotch could offer was too feeble to prevent his seizure of the castles of Edinburgh and Perth. So overwhelming indeed was his military strength, and so rapid his movements, that the Scotch nobility were easily overthrown and terrorized, many of them, including Baliol, making their submission, even going so far as to renounce their allegiance to their own country, and swearing fealty to the oppressor. The victorious Edward then marched in triumph to Aberdeen and Elgin without resistance, in the comfortable assurance that the obstinate Scot was finally subdued. His triumph, however, was doomed to be of short duration, for there now appeared upon the scene the two doughty champions, Robert Bruce and William Wallace, who, by almost incredible prowess, were able completely to reverse the deplorable conditions under which their country groaned, and, by the crowning victory of Bannockburn, gave the *coup de grace* to the ambitious designs of the English king. This memorable battle, unfortunately, led to no very lengthened cessation of hostilities.

Innumerable forays began to cross the Border to plunder and torment the enemy in every way, until raiding gradually developed into organised Border warfare. The game of plunder and reprisal became the chief occupation of the male inhabitants on both sides of the Border. Hatred of the English was almost the religion of the Border Scot, and to slaughter and spoil him of his belongings became the raider's highest conception of patriotism.

The leading spirit on the Scottish border following this stormy period was Scott of Buccleuch. He it was who might be called, if not the founder, at least the earliest organiser of raiding as a regular occupation, and under his banner the northern counties of

England were made to pay dearly for the Sack of Berwick and other foul deeds of the Edwards. Nor can Buccleuch be blamed for utilising the only materials and adopting the only methods available to avenge the wrongs inflicted upon his country. He joined with the leading lords and chieftains in a permanent alliance for the defence of the Border which, in time, grew to such formidable proportions as to create that extraordinary *imperium in imperio* which so often set the authority of the Crown at defiance.

Within their own domains these chiefs lived and ruled like independent sovereigns, the only effective soldiers in the realm being those absolutely under their command. Any law of which they disapproved they ignored or set at defiance, fearing neither God nor Devil, and obeying the government only so far as it suited their own advantage. In spite of all this independence they were, however, loyal and patriotic. The typical chief or leader was a personage proud of his pedigree and knightly in his bearing, knowing how to conduct himself on occasion with all the dignity and chivalry of a gentleman of honour, and these lofty airs were understood and admired even among the meanest of his retainers. Though the evil conditions under which they lived could not fail to be productive of many untameable spirits, wild beyond the reach of any civilising agency, still the clans as a whole were not without germs of respectability. In spite of their occupation as reivers they held in abhorrence many of the usual vices of the common criminal; for example, although the heinous crime of fire raising was not even a punishable offence, yet perjury or treachery incurred the penalty of death, and nothing was more remarkable than the raiders' scrupulous fidelity and trust in the pledged word.

Sir Ralph Sadler says 'their word was true as steel, and though they would plunder without compunction, yet would they never betray any man who had trusted in them for all the gold in France or Scotland.'

Unfortunately, as we shall see further on, there were occasionally serious violations of this excellent characteristic, but when any member of a clan was found guilty of the offence of breaking his pledge the punishment was stern and merciless. On such occasions the injured party usually appeared at the meeting of the Warden's Court or any other large assemblage of the people with the glove of the accused fixed upon the point of a long lance. This was considered the greatest insult to the whole clan, who, on being satisfied of the culprit's guilt, put him to death so as to clear away the stain of baseness from their name.

The raider was usually well mounted and armed with lance and spear, a steel cap upon his head, a jack slung over his shoulder, and a pistol at his belt.

'The Scots are a bold and hardy race', says Froissart, 'and much inured to war; when they make their invasions into England they march as much as twenty four leagues by night and day without a halt. The Knights and Squires are mounted on large bay horses, the common people on little Galloways. They bring no carriages with them on account of the mountains they have to pass in Northumberland, neither do they carry with them any provisions of bread or wine, for their habits of sobriety are such in time of war, that they will live a long time on flesh half sodden, without bread, and they drink the river water without wine. They have therefore no occasion for pots and pans, for they dress the flesh of their cattle in the skins after they have taken them off, and, being sure to find plenty of them in the country which they invade, they carry none with them; under the flaps of his saddle each man carries a broad plate of metal, behind the saddle a little bag of oat meal.'

Those leaders were held in the highest estimation

whose accurate knowledge of locality enabled them to guide their horsemen safely through the bewildering wastes and moss hags which abounded along the Border, on those dark and misty nights which were usually deemed the fittest for the intended foray.

They usually sallied forth at the dead of night in companies of forty or fifty, stealing quietly away almost without a sound, or a word above a whisper, wending their way by lonely paths known only to themselves and concealing themselves by day in some sheltered hollow or ravine, where their horses could feed unseen. When night closed in they again resumed their stealthy pace, rarely making their attack in open day. If their enemy chanced to be on the watch or had timely warning of the reivers' approach a fierce combat ensued, the leaders boldly singling each other out for a beard to beard encounter. If, on the other hand, the enemy had the misfortune to be caught napping probably all his cattle would be driven forth and the darkness of night turned into day by the blaze of his burning homestead before he had well recovered from his surprise.

All the great families on both sides of the border, Scotts, Elliots, Grahams, Armstrongs, Johnstons, Maxwells, Forsters, Fenwicks, Musgraves and many others were skilled experts in the great game, but this in no way disqualified them from holding office under the crown as Wardens and Magistrates even after their offences had become notorious.

Under such extraordinary circumstances there need be little surprise that cattle stealing ceased to be considered a crime, or even discreditable in the eyes of the inhabitants. Besides, cattle were captured and recaptured with such frequency, and the herds were so mixed and confused, that all trace of original ownership was lost.

If a father or a son were hanged for the offence of cattle lifting, it brought no more stain upon the family than if he had accidentally perished in a snow-storm. It was merely looked upon as an unlucky casualty in the battle of life, and was not infrequently associated with some circumstance of exceptional daring, which greatly augmented the prestige of the surviving kindred. It will readily be seen, then, that the Border raider of the sixteenth century was entirely unlike any other marauder to be found in either England or Scotland, for, in addition to his raiding occupation, he was also a kind of guerilla warrior, guarding the only land frontier at no cost to the crown, and, although not officially recognised as a military force, the government had good reason to be thankful for his services on many a fateful field. So long as his loyalty and patriotism were beyond suspicion, the crown willingly condoned his contempt of law and order, and never bestowed a thought upon the improvement of his moral and economic condition.

CHAPTER II

PRIMITIVE COURTS OF JUSTICE

IN the absence of settled laws, disorders, at times, became so rampant on the Border as to compel the government to send punitive expeditions to enforce obedience, especially among the wild Armstrongs of Liddesdale. But these efforts were usually so intermittent and ineffective as to produce greater disorders than those the government tried to cure. Frequently numbers were hanged for deeds done by the order of their lord, while he continued in full enjoyment of the royal favour, with head erect and conduct unchallenged. Such expeditions were never regarded by the people as an assize for the punishment of the guilty and the protection of the innocent; on the contrary, their coming struck the whole community with terror, for all past experience had taught the people that government invasions—ostensibly for the redress of wrongs—were really raids upon a large scale, where booty was the first consideration. The fact of the possession of a large herd of cattle or other movable stock, instead of being taken as an evidence of prosperity and good citizenship, was enough, without further enquiry, to seal the doom of the owner. Meanwhile the real transgressors, the freebooters and outlaws, easily escaped to the hills on the first sound of alarm, where they remained unmolested, as the military had no desire to run the risk of an ambush among the rocks and ravines of Upper Liddesdale. The most notable of these punitive invasions were those under the command of Douglas, Earl of Angus. The earliest, in 1525, was directed against the Armstrongs, especially the notorious house of Whitehaugh, when Sim Armstrong and twelve of his kindred were captured, along with 600 cattle, 3000 sheep, and 500 goats. The prisoners were carried to Edinburgh, where they were long detained, but ultimately released on giving security for their good behaviour.

The second was in July, 1526, but historians differ as to the success of this expedition; some affirm that Angus was obliged to retire from Jedburgh after three days, and others state that a considerable number of freebooters were apprehended and executed.

The third expedition was in the spring of 1527, when Angus succeeded in penetrating into Liddesdale, where he killed seventeen, hanged twelve, and carried many others to Edinburgh to be executed.

The fourth was in June following, when most of the Armstrongs submitted, giving hostages for their good behaviour.

The fifth was early in the year 1528, but having failed to induce the Kers of Ferniehurst to co-operate with him, Angus was forced to retire.

The sixth occurred shortly after, when he again marched to Jedburgh, but there is no reliable record as to the success attending this last effort[1].

The natural result of these indiscriminate raids was to drive the plundered inhabitants who were fortunate enough to escape with their lives, into the ranks of the outlaws.

Increased disorders, disease, and famine followed in the wake of all the Angus invasions; for his barbarous policy was, as he frequently declared, to starve the outlaws into submission by depriving the whole community of the means of subsistence.

As might have been supposed, when food became scarce within the raided district the outlaws extended

[1] Armstrong's *Liddesdale*, p. 253.

their operations far into both England and Scotland, spreading the evil over districts hitherto beyond the wave of their activities.

The most notable feature of the rule among the clans was the system of blackmail, or protection money, paid to the superior lord or chief. In modern times we attach a widely different meaning to the term than did our Border ancestors. Blackmail nowadays has come to mean the base attempt to extort money by threats of injury to the character or violence to the person, but in ancient times it only meant payment of rent, or fees in kind, such payments being called black rent or mail in contradistinction to payment in coin, which was called white rent. This blackmail was paid as willingly and punctually as the ordinary payment of the rent of a farm, for it was by this system that a man's life and property were reasonably well ensured. The chief who received this tribute bound himself not only to refrain from plundering the contributor, but he also undertook to protect him from all others; moreover, he was pledged to recover and restore to him all the cattle or other goods carried off in the raids.

For general government the Border was divided into three districts, the east, west, and middle marches, and over each a warden was appointed representing the Crown. These officers had power to command the attendance of all nobles and chieftains for the administration of justice, the settlement of quarrels, and the regulation of questions of ransom. They also enforced the laws of march treason. Their decisions were without appeal, and to this court alone could the victim of oppression apply for redress of any wrong, however great.

The president was usually a nobleman of the highest standing, and his colleagues were men of rank and importance—indeed, if high-sounding names were a sure guarantee for the pure administration of justice, the dwellers in this interesting land had reason for measureless content. Unfortunately for the frailty of high-born humanity, we find that these judges, like Sir John Falstaff, had little hesitation in setting their nobility aside when there was the slightest whisper of plunder in the wind. Few of them came into court with clean hands, and on many occasions gentlemen with historic names and titles were notoriously well known to have shared in the very booty which was the subject of their grave magisterial nvestigation.

A day of truce was held every month, when the wardens met, the date and place of meeting being proclaimed in all the market towns throughout the marches. Notice was also sent to the lords, knights, squires, and gentlemen commanding them, along with a sufficient number of their servants and tenants, to repair, the night before, and attend upon the warden on the day of truce[1].

There was considerable formality between the two great cavalcades, English and Scotch. When they came within sight of each other a halt was called and four gentlemen on the English side, dismounting approached the Scotch with ceremonious deference and respect for the purpose of demanding of their warden that assurance might be kept until sunrise on the following day. Assurance having been given by the Scotch warden, four gentlemen passed from the Scotch to the English side to demand like assurance from them. These preliminary ceremonies and precautions having been duly observed the two parties met, formed their court, and began their duties.

Here it may be mentioned that the warden's powers were very extensive and greatly coveted by the leading nobility. He had power to call out the full force of the Wardenry for the purpose of invading the opposite kingdom or resenting an attack in time of war, and as representing the Crown he

[1] Armstrong's *Liddesdale*, p. 18.

held judiciary powers enabling him to try all subjects accused of offences against the laws of their country He also bound himself to expel all thieves and oppressors, and to prevent their returning to his Wardenry, and in order to enable him to control the more turbulent members of the clans, all nobles, barons, landholders, and masters were bound to appear before him with their tenants and servants when their names happened to appear in the 'dittay' on a complaint of their countrymen [1].

The warden had thus the opportunity, of which he freely availed himself, of oppressing those persons with whom he was at enmity when they had the misfortune to be brought before him, and also of favouring and screening his kinsmen and friends when they happened to be accused or found guilty of crimes. His decisions were therefore at times hotly resented, and even his life so endangered as to compel him to resign, finding he could no longer preside in safety. The tribunal was altogether corrupt and haphazard, and yet it exercised an authority in which the people seemed to acquiesce, though they were well aware that their judges were often hopelessly at variance with each other even to the length of deadly feuds, and that the fate of a prisoner was frequently less dependent on his proved guilt or innocence than upon the lord whom he served or the clan to which he belonged.

The proceedings began by the selection of six gentlemen from each side to act as the jury. No murderer, traitor, fugitive, or infamous person could bear office or give evidence, but only good and lawful men deserving of credit. The next formality was the warden's oath. These officers stood up facing each other and swore as follows: 'By the high God that reigneth above all kings and realms and to whom all Christians owe obedience, I shall, in His name, do exercise and use my office without respect of person

[1] Balfour's *Practicks*, p. 599.

malice, favour or affection, diligently, according to my vocation, or the charge that I bear under God and my prince, and I shall do justice upon all complaints presented unto me upon every person complained upon under this rule, and when any complaint is referred unto me to clear or fyle and deliver upon my honour, I shall search, enquire and redress the same at my utmost power, and that, if I shall happen, in so doing to quit and absolve the persons complained upon as clean and innocent, yet if I shall, in any way, get sure knowledge of the very offender, I shall declare him foul of the offence, and make lawful redress and delivery thereof, albeit the offender be not named in the complaint'[1]. This oath was made solemnly once every year, at the first meeting after midsummer, 'to put the wardens in the better remembrance of their duties and to place the fear of God in their hearts'.

All formalities having been complied with, the trials of prisoners began. The case of the prisoner last arrested took precedence, and when the bill came up, it might be acquitted summarily on the honour of the lord warden, but if it were afterwards found that he had decided upon imperfect information, the complainant was free to prosecute a new bill. The case was then submitted to a jury, who, after much wrangling, cleaned or fouled the bill at their discretion, writing the word 'fouled' or 'cleared' on the margin. There was a third way of dealing with bills, mentioned by Sir Robert Bowes, who says: 'The assize of Scotland, notwithstanding their oath, decline to find a true bill against a Scotchman upon an Englishman's complaint, unless it could be supported by the evidence of one of their own countrymen, openly given in court, or secretly whispered to the warden. Although the matter were ever so notoriously known by the English witnesses, their evidence would not serve to secure a conviction.' Frequently there were bogus bills

[1] *Leges Marchiarum.*

presented by persons pretending they had been
robbed when nothing had been stolen from them,
and others, who had really been robbed, put in such
preposterous claims for their cattle and gear that had
such been admitted, the complainants would have
been enriched by the loss of their property. This
practice became so serious that commissioners were
appointed to draw up a scale of prices, fixing the
maximum amount which could be recovered for all
kinds of live stock. There was also considerable
difficulty in securing the attendance of offenders who
were men of rank and power, and whose large
following made it impossible to retain them in
custody. In such cases bonds were usually taken
from the kinsmen or allies of the accused, binding
them to enter him prisoner within the iron gates of
the warden's castle, or else to make him forthcoming
when wanted. He against whom a bill was twice
fouled was liable to the penalty of death, or if he
attempted to escape after being lawfully delivered
over to the opposite warden, he was liable to the
death penalty, or otherwise to be dealt with at the
warden's discretion[1]. When all bills had been either
fouled or cleared, those who had been found guilty of
march treason were brought up for sentence. The lord
warden then addressed himself to those officers whose
duty it was to see the execution carried out in the
following words: 'I command you in the King's
name that ye see execution done upon the prisoners
according to the law of the marches at your peril.'
Then, addressing the prisoners, he pronounced
sentence as follows: 'Ye that are adjudged by the
law of the realm to die, remember that ye have a
short time to live in this world, therefore earnestly
call to God with penitent hearts, for mercy and for
forgiveness of your sinful lives; repent that ye have
broken God's commandments, and be sorry therefor,
and for that ye did not fear the breach and danger of

[1] *Border Antiquities*, p. 108.

the law, therefore your bodies must suffer the pain of death provided to satisfy the reward of your fact in this world: yet the salvation of your soul's health for the world to come stands in the great mercy of Almighty God. Wherefore do ye earnestly repent and ask mercy for your sins now when ye are living. Put your trust to be saved by the merits of Christ's passion, and think in your hearts if ye were able to recompense them ye have offended, ye would do it, and where you are not able ask forgiveness. Have such faith in God's mercy as Durmas the thief and man-murderer had that hung at Christ's right hand when He suffered His passion for the redemption of mankind, whose faith was so great he should be saved, his sins were remitted, and, though he had but short time for repentance, yet he enjoyed heaven. Therefore despair not of God's mercy though your sins be great, for God's mercy extendeth over all His works. Forsake the vanities of this world, and comfort you in heavenly things. Doubt not but if ye do so ye shall inherit everlasting joy in the kingdom of heaven. And thus I commit you to the mercy of God, wishing your deaths may be an example to all parents to bring up their children in the fear of God and obedience to the laws of the realm'[1].

With these words ringing in their ears the condemned were led forth to immediate execution, and the startling reflection forces itself upon the mind how the warden, when himself a guilty promoter and secret partner in those crimes against God and the realm, could dare to pronounce, with such solemn sermonising, a death sentence upon poor men for deeds that he had so often himself committed. There was no great difference between the guilt of the warden and that of the prisoner beyond the fact that the one was strong and the other weak.

The business of the court being over the wardens retired, taking a formal and friendly leave of each

[1] *Leges Marchiarum*, p. 124.

PRIMITIVE COURTS OF JUSTICE

other. Occasionally these wardens' court days were disturbed by serious brawls and bloodshed. In the month of July, 1585, on a day of truce, Lord Russell was shot dead by some unknown hand, an event which caused a prolonged and angry altercation between the two governments; but, on the whole, the system, with all its defects, worked as well as any other form of procedure which could have been devised in those rude times.

Many of the laws of the marches were very peculiar, and were always sternly enforced. If a Scotchman entered England without a safe conduct, anyone was at liberty to apprehend him and bring him before the English warden, who, being satisfied that he was a lawful prisoner, would deliver him again to his captor, who was entitled to exact a ransom for his freedom. By mutual agreement, very serious offenders were run down by what was known as 'hot trod'. When a malefactor of this class fled from one country to the other, the warden of either realm might pursue him with 'hot trod, hue and cry, hound and horn', anywhere unchecked until the offender was captured. If a man pursued a cattle-stealer and captured him, he was not only permitted to behead him upon the spot, but he became entitled to the whole of the stolen animals to whomsoever they belonged by right of conquest, and his they remained so long as he could retain them.

Raids were frequently made, less for plunder than for revenge, of some ancient wrong or insult, which many years of smouldering wrath had ripened into a deadly feud which continued from one generation to another, in some cases long after the circumstances of the original quarrel had been forgotten by both parties. A famous feud arose between Scott of Buccleuch and Charlton of Hesleyside (regarding the possession of an ancient sword to which both laid claim), and led to many years of bad blood and to the loss of innumerable lives.

But one of the greatest feuds of ancient times was that between the Armstrongs and the Grahams arising from jealousy of each other's strength in the debateable land, and which, from the large force of fighting men belonging to each clan, gave the government considerable uneasiness. All hopes of a peaceful settlement between these angry clans having been abandoned, the King consented to a trial of their strength in the open field as the only probable settlement of their deadly quarrel. On receipt of the royal sanction, the two clans gathered up their whole fighting strength for the great duel, which was to decide the question of future masterdom in Canonbie.

They met on the banks of the Esk, near Hollows, where the encounter was prolonged and bloody. Great numbers were slain on both sides, but finally the Armstrongs were victorious, the Grahams being driven down Eskdale over the border into Cumberland, and probably from this event may be traced their first settlement in England.

These deadly feuds made it at all times dangerous to assemble the inhabitants before the warden's court, where the Border laws were administered. The lords and chiefs on these occasions were commanded under threats of outlawry to give security that they would abstain from fighting during the fifteen days of the court's sitting, the penalty for disobedience in such a case being death.

Sometimes even the bitterest of these family feuds were quenched by a romantic surrender on both sides to the loftier claims of love. It not infrequently happened that a chief or leader won the heart of the daughter or sister of his hereditary foe, or a bride of great importance in the enemy's clan, an event which never failed to touch the chivalrous instincts of the Borderer and soften the animosities on both sides.

When all the grievances and wrongs of bygone

days were dismissed from the hearts of the clansmen in this delightful fashion, and the reunion celebrated with great rejoicings, it was customary for both sides to join in a pilgrimage to some noted shrine, there to pray for the repose of the souls of all those who had been slain on both sides, and to cement the pledge of future alliance and goodwill.

These feuds added greatly to the fierce character of the raiding expeditions, especially those between clans on opposite sides of the Border. They were mainly to blame for the continued sense of insecurity along the frontier even in times of international peace, when it was necessary to maintain as vigilant an outlook upon each other's movements as in times of actual war. Numerous beacons were always in readiness to light up upon the signal of alarm. On the Scottish side of the Border these bale-fires were placed on Trail Trow Hill, Cowden, above Castlemilk, Drysdail, Skenton in Applegarth parish, Brown Hill, The Blees in Wamphray parish, Kindalknock in the parish of Johnston, Gallow Hill, Moffat, Wardlaw, Pittarahill, Mallow Hill, Corswainton, and several other heights further north. They were all under the direct supervision of the Sheriff of Nithsdale, the Steward of Annandale, and the Steward of Kirkcudbright, who were held responsible for their efficiency in the hour of need.

On the English side similar beacons were placed on Black Coombe, Boothill, Muncaster Fell, St. Bees Head, Workington Hill, Moot Bay, Skiddaw, Sundale Top, Carlisle Castle, Lingyclose-head, Beacon Hill, Penrith, Brampton Mote, Stanmore, Orton Scar, Farlton Knot, Whinfell, and Hard Knot.

The peculiar situation of the debateable land lent itself greatly to systematic raiding, forming, as it did, something of the character of a small buffer state between the two kingdoms claimed by both, but pending the settlement of that ancient and endless dispute, allowed to be beyond the jurisdiction of either. It was ruled by the Grahams until their great defeat passed it over to the Armstrongs of the house of Mangerton, under Johnie of Gilnockie.

During the earlier part of the sixteenth century repeated efforts were made by England to obtain possession of it by force of arms. Again and again Lord Dacre of Gillisland scourged it with fire and sword, and if we may accept his own account of his success in the business of devastation, its ruin ought to have been irretrievable and final.

In the year 1527, on being reprehended by the Council in London for his lack of capacity, and of enterprise in reducing and annexing this much desired belt of territory, he defended himself as follows:

'For one cattle taken by the Scots, I have taken scores, and for every sheep I have taken hundreds, and as for the townships and houses within the Scottish marches, I can assure your Lordships that I have caused to be burned and destroyed six times more towns and houses within the same season than the Scotch have done to us, as I shall prove. All along the vale of the Liddle and many miles up the river Ewes, together with Annan and thirty-nine other townships, I have utterly destroyed.'

He concludes his report with a minute account 'of the extensive cornfields, and the many hundreds of ploughs he has burned and laid waste'[1].

Probably this catalogue of his boastful deeds of rapine was exaggerated to impress the Council with his meritorious energy in executing the duties of his office as warden of the English marches.

If the debateable land had been so completely swept, and reduced to the howling wilderness his words imply, then the recuperative energies of the Canonbie men must have been little less than superhuman, for we find that immediately following this

[1] Quoted by Sir H. Maxwell in his *Dumfries and Galloway*, pp. 159, 160.

crushing invasion Johnie and Simon Armstrong were not only in possession of every inch of the debateable land, but were at the head of a well-armed force, hurling defiance at Lord Dacre and his well-trained military equipments.

CHAPTER III

LORD MAXWELL

BEHIND the Armstrongs stood one of the ablest and most unscrupulous lords in Scotland, namely, Lord Maxwell, by whom they were secretly encouraged to fight. He was a born conspirator, and at this time the crafty warden of the Scottish western marches. A treaty of peace had been signed between Maxwell and Lord Cumberland, by which the conquest of the debateable land was left entirely to the discretion of the English, and would no longer be opposed by the forces of the Scottish Wardenry. This treaty was merely a trick to encourage Dacre to cross the Border, where he would find himself entangled in a well-devised ambush and cut to pieces by the Armstrongs and their allies, of whose strength Dacre seems to have been surprisingly ignorant.

Believing that the Scottish warden's neutrality was secured under the treaty, and the way open for a great attack upon the Armstrongs, Dacre advanced into Canonbie with his finely equipped army of 2000 men. Along with him were Sir John Radcliffe, Sir Christopher Dacre, and William Musgrave, all commanders of note, against whose military skill and great powers the untrained mosstrooper would be likely to contend in vain.

Their plan of invasion was cunningly devised to throw the Armstrongs off their guard, and to fall upon them where least expected, the objective being the stronghold of Gilnockie on the Esk, four miles below Langholm. Unfortunately for Dacre, his intentions were revealed to the Armstrongs, who made their dispositions accordingly. Dacre was allowed to wend his way northward, without a sign of resistance, in pursuance of his well-considered plan.

He continued to advance without sight or sound of an enemy until he found himself within view of Gilnockie. Here he was surprised by a sudden and overwhelming rush of clansmen, who seemed to spring from every bush and rock. A terrible fight ensued, raging round Hollows Tower, which was soon in flames. Inferior though the Armstrongs were in numbers, their skill, daring, and dash soon overbalanced the more regular military methods of Dacre's army, which began to waver, and finally broke and fled. The Cumbrians were completely defeated, and driven, a disorderly mob, down the valley of the Esk. Great numbers were slain, and so hot was the pursuit of the victorious Armstrongs, that both Kirk-Andrews and Netherby were destroyed before the day closed in.

Dacre was deeply mortified at this crushing defeat of his well-trained military force by an army of freebooters, whose prowess he had affected to treat with scorn. By way of excuse and explanation of the humiliating disaster, he boldly accused Lord Maxwell, in his report to the Privy Council, of treacherous connivance with the Armstrongs, and, further, that his secretly made treaty and his friendly assurances were only tricks to induce the Cumbrian troops to march into an ambush which he had himself helped the Armstrongs to plan.

Possibly Dacre was not far wrong in this surmise, as Maxwell seemed in no way anxious to clear his character by a denial of so serious a charge, but rather lent likelihood to it by the vehement expression of his indignation at the burning of Hollows Tower, for which he claimed compensation, alleging that it was within the lordship of Esk, and not within the debateable land to which Dacre's activities were by the treaty confined. On the other hand, Dacre claimed for the burning of Netherby, and after a prolonged and acrimonious dispute in the Warden's Court, the subject was allowed to drop[1].

This crowning victory over the English warden raised the fame and the popularity of Johnie Armstrong of Gilnockie to a height which no Border chief had ever before attained. He had baffled all the Cumbrian raids for years, and had finally inflicted a defeat upon a large scale against troops led by three warriors of distinction.

In seeking to excuse himself to the Privy Council for the disastrous blow he had suffered at Hollows, Dacre accused Ritchie Graham of Netherby of having betrayed his plan of campaign to the Armstrongs, notwithstanding the fact that Netherby (his home) had been burned to the ground by them. Graham's connivance seems to have been conjectured merely on the ground of his relationship with Gilnockie by marriage. Upon this feeble assumption, however, he was arrested and confined in Carlisle Castle. While awaiting his trial he managed to escape, and fled into Scotland where he was joined by his relatives and a large number of retainers, all of whom were cordially received and entertained by Lord Maxwell.

In no long time the real traitor who had been in secret league with Gilnockie was discovered to have been one Storey, a landowner in Cumberland, and a man of some importance. After his arrest he admitted his guilt, but managed to escape from prison, and fled into Northumberland.

For the great wrong done to the Grahams by Dacre's accusation restitution was made by dividing the lands of the traitor Storey between the Grahams of Mote and the Grahams of Netherby[2].

For some time after the defeat of Dacre comparative

[1] Cottonian MSS. *Caligula*, 6. 11 f. 378 and 379.
[2] *Caligula*, 6. x. f. 180.

peace reigned upon the Western Marches, and ancient animosities so far subsided that the Armstrongs were accorded the privilege of attending the Carlisle market, an advantage they greatly appreciated. This was a step in the right direction, likely to promote friendly intercourse and to accustom the people to methods of dealing more in accordance with civilisation than the old game of killing and thieving. For some unexplained reason, however, the restless, headstrong Dacre persuaded Cardinal Wolsey to allow him to withdraw this great boon, and once more the Border was in an uproar.

This sudden exclusion from the market without warning or reason assigned roused the greatest resentment among the Armstrongs, who forthwith set about the organisation of a raid into England upon a great scale.

The whole strength of the clan, including Mangerton, Sim of Whitehaugh, and their allies the Elliots, Nicksons, Croziers, and others, entered Bewcastle by night and captured an important tenant of Lord Dacre, who, with the whole of his cattle and goods, was speedily on the road to Liddesdale. It chanced that Dacre was in the immediate neighbourhood at the time, and himself directed a vigorous pursuit, which gained so rapidly upon the spoil-encumbered Armstrongs that they were overtaken within a mile of Kershope. The English, seeing the apparently small number of the reivers, galloped boldly to the attack, and in spite of past experience thought precautions unnecessary. Presently they found, to their dismay, that they had cantered into a well-planned ambush. The Armstrongs sprang upon them in flank and rear, defeated them, and took 40 prisoners, 11 of whom they promptly hanged.

This cunningly planned system of ambush by which the Liddesdale men overthrew their enemies was a great feature in Border warfare, and subsequently we shall find it was practised with consummate skill on more occasions than one.

Lord Dacre, finding himself again disgraced and overthrown by the Armstrongs, turned his wrath upon the commander of the horse garrison of Bewcastle, whom he denounced for having not only failed to join his countrymen in the 'hot trod,' but of having failed to give warning either of the in-coming or the out-going of the marauders.

So powerless was Dacre in dealing with his northern enemies, that we find him at last obliged to appeal direct to Wolsey to use his influence in so small a matter as the exchange of prisoners. One of his most important servants, Miles Hilton, had been detained a prisoner over the Border for more than a year, and as he found it beyond the power of Lord Bothwell, the keeper of Liddesdale, or even of the Scottish King himself to procure his release, he begged the Cardinal to negotiate his exchange for one of the Nicksons he held in custody.

Commissioners were at length appointed by King Henry, and were duly instructed by Wolsey. In these instructions it was stated that 'attempts at sundry times within the last truce had been by the Scots committed against the English realm without any redress. Further, that the wardens themselves, as was notoriously known, who had been appointed to execute justice, had themselves been the principal transgressors, abettors, recetters, and procurers of divers of the same attempts. And that if it was found that by reason of the great disobedience and division on the Borders of Scotland that the Scots would not make redress for all, to endeavour to obtain redress for as many complaints as possible, particularly for offences against the servants of Lord Dacre, who, in pursuing certain malefactors of Scotland had been fraudulently brought into a great ambushment of the Scots, by whom they were afterwards shamefully murdered and slain, which crime, if unpunished, would not only encourage the Scots, but discourage the English'[1].

The Armstrongs of Whitehaugh were, during the greater part of the sixteenth century, the most fearless of Border aggressors, treating the authority of King and warden alike with indifference, and ever ready to take the field against any odds. To quote the words of Lord Ernest Hamilton, 'Sim the lord was the third of those lairds of Whitehaugh who can only be described as a race of fiends who kept the Borderland in a state of terror for several decades. His father and grandfather had died on the Haribie with their necks in a noose, as became lairds of that name, and he rarely rode forth but he left gouts of blood on the door step of his victim, with a weeping widow and wondering children standing by.'

In the spring of 1529 an ultimatum was sent to the Armstrongs from the English government allowing them a fixed period within which to make restitution for various high crimes and misdemeanours, but Magnus reported to King Henry 'that the Armstrongs, led by Sim the lord, had answered presumptuously that they would not be ordered either by the King of Scots, their sovereign lord, nor by the King of England, but after such manner as their fathers had used before them. And further, that the Armstrongs had boasted of having destroyed fifty-two parish churches, in addition to their innumerable raids into England.' For this deplorable hostility to their sovereign, James very justly blamed the impolitic severity of the Earl of Angus.

His six atrocious raids had extinguished their loyalty, and driven them on to a reckless defiance of authority. King James was at this time embittered against Angus, from whose custody he had only recently escaped, the Earl having fled to the English Court, where he resided in exile, in

[1] Armstrong's *Liddesdale*.

favour with King Henry. James accused Angus of having, under the pretence of checking the Border outlaws, secretly encouraged and maintained the worst of them, to such an extent that not only had they greatly increased in number, but by their extensive robberies, had amassed great riches, and were now so far out of dread of their sovereign lord, that their reformation without English help had become impossible.

It was finally resolved to throw the whole responsibility for their reduction to obedience upon Lord Bothwell, keeper of Liddesdale, now dwelling at Hermitage Castle, in the centre of the Armstrong country. He was forced to undertake their subjection, and to compel them to make redress for past wrongs, upon pain of forfeiture of the lordship.

The unruly barons of the West Marches also entered into negotiations, and as a first condition of good behaviour, procured for themselves and their tenants a remission of their past sins, on their pledging themselves to keep good rule within their bounds, and to deliver up to the King's authority all persons accused of murder, theft, treason, and other deadly crimes, on fifteen days' warning. Each baron who was answerable for any criminal within his bounds, undertook to expel him, along with his wife and children, and in the event of his returning, and being suffered to remain for twelve hours, the baron became answerable for any crime the culprit might thereafter commit. He also undertook that should any rebel, 'being at the horn', enter his domains, he would rise with his people and slay, or drive him forth; and if he failed in the honest performance of these duties, he was content to abide a trial by assize, and agreed that if proved guilty, he would be liable to punishment by death, confiscation of his lands, or otherwise, a complete restitution of all the goods stolen by the malefactor. The warden, Lord Maxwell, also bound himself, in presence of the King, to maintain law and order throughout the dales of Esk, Wauchope, and Ewes, as well as within the Sheriffdom of Dumfries, and the Stewartry of Annandale, excepting those lords and barons who had entered into their own special bonds.

All these pledges and undertakings were of little avail, however, and the peace was of short duration. Again the Armstrongs of Whitehaugh, in defiance of all treaties, broke loose. Crossing the Border more than a hundred strong, they raided the cattle from a place called Byrkshaws, and left the place in flames.

They were swiftly pursued by Nicholas Ridley, a retainer of the Earl of Northumberland, with a considerable troop of horse; but they, as usual, followed too far, ultimately dropping into a skilfully planned ambush, where Ridley and eighteen of his men were captured and hanged. Northumberland complained to King James, especially protesting against the inactivity of Lord Bothwell, who was responsible for the conduct of the Armstrongs, but whose guilty connivance was more than suspected. Again the whole Border rang with quarrels and disputations which roused King James to take the Border question into his own hands. By his first step he showed what value he placed upon the recently given solemn bonds and promises of his nobility. He directed Bothwell, Home, Maxwell, Johnston, Buccleuch, Drumlanrig, Wamfray, Ker, and several others to be arrested and placed in ward, where they were to remain during His Majesty's pleasure, at their own expense, under forfeiture of life, lands, and goods. Meanwhile, James arranged to advance in person with a large following of his trusted nobles to call the marauders to account, and to restore the Border to a state of tranquillity.

He called upon all lords and substantial gentry within the bounds of Edinburgh, Stirling, Perth,

Linlithgow, and other counties, to meet him at Edinburgh, on the 26th of June, 1530, along with their retainers, armed and victualled for forty days, in order that they might accompany him wherever it should please him to pass towards the Border, and not depart until his return under pain of life, lands, and goods.

It was also ordered that the wardens of the West and Middle Marches, all of whom were under arrest, should send their deputies to the Border to meet the wardens of England.

When all arrangements were completed, King James started on this memorable expedition at the head of a force of 8000 men, passing through Tweeddale and by way of St. Mary's Loch. On his way he turned aside to make a friendly call upon William Cockburn of Henderland, a warrior of note. The interview was of the briefest, and when the King left, Cockburn's body was dangling from a tree in the presence of his young and weeping wife, a tragedy believed to have inspired the beautiful ballad of 'The Border Widow.'

> My love he built me a bonnie bower,
> And clad it a' wi' lilye flour,
> A brawer bower ye ne'er did see,
> Than my true love he built for me.

> There came a man by middle day,
> He spied his sport, and went away ;
> And brought the King, that very night,
> Who brake my bower and slew my knight.

> He slew my knight, to me sae dear,
> He slew my knight, and poin'd his gear ;
> My servants all for life did flee,
> And left me in extremitie.

> I sewed his sheet, making my mane ;
> I watched the corpse myself alane ;
> I watched his body, night and day,
> No living creature came that way.

I took his body on my back,
And whiles I gaed and whiles I sat ;
I digged a grave, and laid him in,
And happ'd him with the sod sae green.

 But think na ye my heart was sair,
 When I laid the moul's on his yellow hair ;
 Oh think na ye my heart was wae,
 When I turned about, awa' to gae ?

Nae living man I'll love again,
Since that my lovely knight was slain ;
Wi' yae lock o' his yellow hair
I'll chain my heart for ever mair.

CHAPTER IV

JOHNIE ARMSTRONG

IT is necessary now to draw more minute attention to Lord Maxwell, who was at this time in close alliance with twelve of the greatest families, among them Douglas of Drumlanrig, Stewart of Garlis, Gordon of Lochinvar, Chartris of Amisfield, and John of Gilnockie, from all of whom he had received bonds of man-rent.

He was the Lord Warden, the Chief Magistrate, and Conservator of the Peace, to whom the community had to look for the honest administration of justice. How he fulfilled his great trust is amusingly related in a Border document. One of his colleagues, Chartris of Amisfield, was proved to have stolen the cattle of one John Partree in an unprovoked foray, purely in search of plunder. Partree claimed redress at the Warden's Court, which gave judgment in his favour, ordering Chartris to restore the poor man's nolt. Such a decision he treated with scorn, admitting freely that he had lifted the man's live stock, but declined to return them on the ground that Partree's premises were within the debateable land, where the jurisdiction of the Court was doubtful [1].

Under these circumstances the only alternative left to the Court was an appeal to the Scottish Commissioners to uphold its judgment. These Commissioners were invested with extensive powers, but not sufficient to settle a cattle transaction in which great men's interests were involved. They were

[1] Armstrong's *Liddesdale*.

obliged meekly to inform the Court that their authority was useless, and that they would be obliged to hold a consultation with the Lord Regent, for, said they, the laird of Amisfield was a very great man, and would not be ruled by any one, besides he had the full support of Lord Maxwell, *who got a share of the stolen cattle himself.* Thus the warden of a Court, accustomed to condemn cattle-stealers to the gallows by scores, in lofty and pious exhortations about their souls' needs in the hour of death, had no hesitation in fouling his hands with the identical crime for which these inferior wretches suffered.

When Lord Maxwell was at the height of his power, the authority of the Crown along the Western Marches almost came to an end. The most imperious orders of the Council were sometimes ignored, and occasionally openly defied.

Repeated summonses were sent to the lords of Eskdale, Ewesdale, and Annandale commanding them to appear before the Council with their pledges, under pain of rebellion. First one date would be named, and none appearing, a second would be fixed, accompanied by still stronger threats of punishment for disobedience. After that a third and a fourth date would be named, but still no compliance or even response could be extorted. Notwithstanding all this open contempt of the Crown, not a single step seems to have been taken to vindicate the King's authority.

Lord Maxwell and his confederates knew that these threats were mere bluster if used at a time when the political situation was critical, for the safety of the kingdom to a great degree rested upon the loyalty of the fighting men of the Border.

This ostentatious defiance was ultimately carried too far, as we shall see, but its immediate effect was to swell the importance of Maxwell in the eyes of the clans, especially when they saw that the government feared and yielded to him on so many occasions.

c

Thus all the conditions lent themselves to the building up of a dangerous and unscrupulous tyranny under which grievous wrongs were committed against individuals, and all redress refused if these wrongs were profitable to the warden and his favourites.

Among his many evil deeds there was one of unusual blackness, in which he incited the Armstrongs to attack his most formidable rival and near relation, the laird of Johnstone, taking advantage of a blood feud which existed between the families of Armstrong and Johnstone, originating in the slaughter of Mickle Sim of Whitehaugh, by Johnstone of that ilk. In arranging the plot against the life of his kinsman, the Lord Warden agreed to lie in ambush, pledging himself to surprise and kill Johnstone with his own hand if he attempted to pursue.

This was the chief whose jealousy had been awakened by the rising fame of Gilnockie, and whose heart was now set upon his destruction. King James the Fifth was too young, too ignorant and inexperienced in Border affairs to understand its many complications, and was easily persuaded by Lord Maxwell and his agents that Johnie Armstrong of Gilnockie was at the root of most of the pressing evils on the Scottish Border, that his rapidly growing wealth and influence were so dangerous to the government that his removal by death was urgently necessary. It was much easier, however, to plot Gilnockie's destruction than to accomplish it. Maxwell knew that if his hand were detected in such a foul conspiracy, notwithstanding his position of warden, the Border would be too hot to hold him. It was widely known, indeed, that the warden's autocratic power rested mainly upon the fidelity of Gilnockie and his great material support, for he was ever true to his bond of man-rent.

King James was also warned of the danger of approaching Canonbie with hostile intent, for there was no military force at the disposal of the Crown

GILNOCKIE TOWER

able to crush the strong league of Border chiefs banded together for mutual aggression and defence.

It was hopeless, therefore, to attempt to beard the lion in his den, but there was another way of slaying him: in point of fact he was lost through the nobility of his own character. It is only fair, however, to record that there is division of opinion among historians in regard to the treachery of Lord Maxwell in the death of Gilnockie, but if all the evidence which has come down to us be fairly weighed, little doubt can be left on the mind that he alone contrived the means by which it became possible of accomplishment.

The unusual readiness with which he and his allies, who were bound to defend Gilnockie, allowed themselves to be placed in ward when James advanced against the Border, and the direct advantage he secured to himself by Gilnockie's death, fixed the guilt upon this cunning knave, whose cruelties and crimes 'have damned his name to eternal fame.'

Notwithstanding the trick by which Gilnockie was separated from his allies, James dared not face him openly on the Border side among his devoted followers, but sought to lure him to his doom by professions of the warmest approval and friendship.

King's agents were sent to advise him of the approaching royal visit, and to invite him to meet his sovereign at Carlinrigg, where he was assured in a letter, written by the King's own hand, that his coming would be most cordially welcomed. Johnie, with his native nobility of character, never doubted the sincerity of his King. Raider though he was, he had no suspicion of the possibility of a baseness in a crowned monarch which even Border reivers would have scorned. In his own simple way he regarded his sovereign as the fountain of honour and the highest ideal of chivalry, one who could never stain his ermine by a deed of treachery, the like of which was punished with death in every Border clan.

So unreserved was his trust that he declined to

ask even for the usual safe conduct, and resolved to show his complete faith in the honour of James. He determined to appear before him with fifty of his select companions entirely unarmed. Moreover, it is worthy of note that Gilnockie's faith in King James was shared by his whole clan, whose delight at the conspicuous extension of the royal favour to their great chief was expressed by loud and prolonged rejoicings throughout the debateable land. Johnie, with his splendidly attired horsemen, rode up Eskdale, and through the town of Langholm, where he received an ovation, and was greeted on all sides with enthusiastic demonstrations of loyalty to James and goodwill to Johnie. The occasion was memorable, and has been charmingly pictured to us by some poet of the time whose name is unknown. The ballad is well known, but no account of Gilnockie can be complete without quotation from it. It is of great length, but the following four verses describe the joyful leave-taking of the warriors:

> Some spieks of lords, some spieks of lairds,
>   And sicklyke men of hie degree,
> Of a gentleman I sing a sang,
>   Sometime called laird of Gilnockie.
>
> The King he writes a loving letter
>   With his ain hand sae tenderly,
> And he hath sent to Johnie Armstrong
>   To come and spiek with him speedily.
>
> The Elliots and Armstrongs did convene,
>   They were a gallant company,
> We'll ride and meet our lawful King,
>   And bring him safe to Gilnockie.
>
> They ran their horses on the Langholm home,
>   They brake their spears with mickle main,
> The ladies luket frae their loft windows,
>   God bring our men well back again.

Having passed the town of Langholm the warriors, full of their joyful anticipations, rode merrily up

Ewesdale, and through the gorge between the hills at Mosspaul, but when they reached a spot somewhere near the modern farmhouse of Linhope, they found themselves suddenly surrounded by large bodies of horsemen who came galloping down from the folds of the hills where they had been ambushed.

The Armstrongs saw no signs of the promised cordial welcome. On the contrary they were closed in upon, taken prisoners, and hurried along to their fate.

Conceptions of honour and fidelity as understood among Border reivers had misled them and brought them defenceless under the angry eyes of one whose will was absolute, and to whom the instincts of pity and chivalry were alike unknown.

The story is full of tragic interest, and has been told by several of the sixteenth century historians. It is related that ' When Gilnockie entered in before the King he came very reverently with his followers very richly apparelled, trusting that in respect that he had come to the King's grace willingly and voluntarily, not being taken or apprehended by the King, he should obtain the more favour.

'But when the King saw him and his men so gorgeous in their apparel, and so many braw men attending his orders, he turned about his face and bade take that tyrant out of his sight, saying, "What wants that knave that a King should have?" But when Johnie perceived that the King kindled in a fury against him, and that he had no hope of his life, notwithstanding many and fair offers he had made him, that is that he should sustain himself and forty gentlemen ever ready to wait upon his Majesty's service, and never to take a penny of Scotland or Scotchmen. Secondly, that there was not a subject in England, Duke, Earl, Lord or Baron, but within a certain day he would bring them dead or alive to his Majesty. Then, seeing no hope of the King's favour towards him, he said very proudly, "I am but a fool to seek grace at a graceless face. But had I known, Sir, that you would have taken my life this day, I should have lived upon the Border side in despite of King Henry and you both, for I know King Harry would weigh down my best horse with gold to know that I had been condemned to die this day " '[1].

And so the deed of shame was consummated by the execution of Gilnockie and his gallant company who were all hung upon the trees growing in the immediate vicinity of the royal camp, ' but Scotland's heart was ne'er sae wae to see sae mony brave men dee.'

' It is worthy of note ', says Bruce Armstrong, ' that there is not in Scotland a single document recording *the trial* of the Armstrongs, and in no known letter in the collection in London is there any allusion to the proceedings of James on the Border during this year.'

We have seen that the inhabitants of Eskdale received a remission as late as the 24th of July, 1529, and as there are many reasons for supposing that no well-founded charge of oppression could have been brought against Gilnockie by his fellow-subjects, there is apparently not a shadow of doubt that he and his followers were not only basely betrayed, but put to death without even the form of a trial.

The murder of Gilnockie was not only an act of the meanest treachery which only the King's youth and ignorance of the political movements going on around him could in some measure excuse, but it was also a blunder, the magnitude of which James was soon to realize. He had struck down the one man of brain and loyalty in the very zenith of his fame and popularity, and at a moment when his unconquerable prowess was most needed in defence of the Border. His long and resolute resistance to all the attempts of the English warden to expel the Armstrongs from Canonbie and the debateable land was the talk of the

[1] *Pitscottie Chron.*, edition 1814, vii. pp. 342, 343.

country. Throughout the Border he was beloved, and we are told that not one truculent act was ever recorded against him. When it became known that he was slain, and basely slain, not only the Border, but all Scotland was roused to indignation, especially when evidence of the planned treachery began to emerge in the settling up of accounts between King James and his pretended prisoner, Lord Maxwell. Only three days after the murders, letters were issued conferring the whole of Gilnockie's lands upon the captive warden, which so stirred the popular resentment that the King was obliged to issue a plea of justification which was as false as his loving letter to Johnie. He made the absurd charge that Gilnockie had secretly conspired to bring the debateable land under obedience to England, he himself being well considered in the service. The best proof of the groundlessness of this charge was to be found in the joy and satisfaction with which the news was hailed in England, when both King Henry and his Border wardens saw at a glance that the most formidable obstacle to a Scotch invasion on the Western side was now beaten down, and that by the King's own hands.

By this deplorable blunder James not only left the debateable land an open gate into his country, but he also lost a splendid opportunity of winning to the side of law and order the refractory spirits on the Border, over whom Gilnockie's strong personality and firm hand had gained a remarkable ascendancy. He was the only man who had risen to the surface, endowed with the essential qualities required for ruling the turbulent and strong-willed clansmen, and though it may seem paradoxical to say it of a professional raider, he was honest according to the lights that were in him, and was not slow to avow it:

> For I loved nathing in all my lyfe
> I dare well say it, but *honesty*,

he tells King James.

No name in the record of Border chivalry has

inspired so much interest as that of Gilnockie, especially among the people of Eskdale, where his memory is held in great respect, and his foul death at Carlinrigg is related by the fireside of farmer and peasant to this day.

So recently as the summer of 1897, quite an imposing assemblage of Borderers took place at Carlinrigg in order to inaugurate a Memorial Stone which had been placed in the wall of the old churchyard where the warriors are interred. The cost of this monument was defrayed by shilling subscriptions, and as none were solicited, the result was a spontaneous offering to the memory of the great Border chief.

The stone is beautifully executed, and bears the following inscription:

Tradition records that near this spot were buried John Armstrong of Gilnockie, and a number of his personal followers, who were treacherously taken and executed by order of King James the Fifth, during his expedition to pacify the Border in July 1530.

> John murdered was at Carlinrigg
> And all his gallant company,
> But Scotland's heart was ne'er sae wae
> To see sae mony brave men dee.

Travellers up the beautiful valley of the Esk are often greatly impressed when, at a well-known turn of the road, near the village of Hollows, they suddenly come in view of the huge, headless skeleton of Gilnockie Tower, with its great brown gables rising high above the surrounding woods, and its square keep, which has stood the assaults of the west winds brattling through its dry ribs for more than four hundred years, yet stately and imposing even in decay.

This was the stronghold of the famous Johnie Armstrong, the highest type of the Border chief, as the men of Whitehaugh were its lowest. Here in 1530 Gilnockie lived and ruled in almost princely independence.

This tower is especially interesting as being the

MEMORIAL STONE ERECTED TO JOHN ARMSTRONG OF GILNOCKIE

most perfect example of a reiver's stronghold which has been preserved to us, though of recent years its mouldering walls have given sad warnings of the final collapse.

The walls are enormously thick, and all within is in a fair state of preservation, especially the keep or dungeon, which occupies most of the ground floor, and the roof of which is arched in grey stone. The entrance is by a low but wide doorway, with carved architraves, and here and there are seen the remains of the heavy iron fittings mouldering in their stone sockets. A spiral stone stair leads to the apartments overhead, and also to the battlements, where the great stone basket, or grid, used for the beacon fires, still surmounts the loftiest of the gables.

It is much to be hoped that this almost perfect example of the stronghold of the bold spirits whose war-horn rang among the Border hills in the days of old, will be found worthy the attention of the Society for the Preservation of Ancient Monuments before its condition has become hopeless.

The tragedy of Carlinrigg has been commemorated by Dr. Leyden in his *Scenes of Infancy* in the following beautiful lines:

> Where rising Teviot joins the Frostylee
> Stands the huge trunk of many a leafless tree,
> No verdant woodbine wreaths their age adorn,
> Bare are their boughs, their gnarled roots uptorn;
> Here shone no sunbeam, fell no summer dew,
> Nor ever grass beneath the branches grew
> Since that bold chief who Henry's power defied,
> True to his country, as a traitor died.
> Yon mouldering cairns by ancient hunters placed
> Where blends the meadow with the marshy waste,
> Mark where the gallant warriors lie—but long
> Their fame shall flourish in the Scotian song,
> The Scotian song, whose deep impulsive tones
> Each thrilling fibre, true to passion owns.
> When soft as gales o'er summer seas that blow
> The plaintive music warbles love-lorn woe,
> Or wild and loud the fierce exulting strain
> Swells its proud notes triumphant o'er the slain.

CHAPTER V

WRATH OF KING HENRY VIII

AFTER the death of Gilnockie the sentiments of loyalty and chivalry began to fade away in the Border clans.

Scotland had not only lost her strongest frontier chief, but the clans under, or in alliance with, him were by his murder so incensed and alienated from their King that reliance could no longer be placed upon their fidelity in the hour of need. The Armstrongs of Liddesdale shook off their allegiance entirely, turning their hand against anyone, English and Scotch alike, they had become pariahs and outcasts fighting for existence.

Large bands of freebooters scoured the country, each fighting and plundering on his own account regardless alike of King or warden. A large company of raiders under the command of Ker of Ferniehirst fell upon the village of Alnham, about 13 miles from Alnwick, which they plundered and burnt, slaying most of the inhabitants, and on the same day pushing on to Newstead, near Bamborough, they captured twenty-six persons, vassals of the Earl of Northumberland, and 200 head of cattle. On the Sunday following the village of Tarbottle was destroyed, after which Ker rode back in safety with his booty to his stronghold in Scotland.

The English Lord Warden—the Earl of Northumberland—greatly incensed at these daring outrages in the vicinity of his own home, began the formation of an army of defence upon a scale of magnitude hitherto unknown upon the Border. Far from being terrorised however, Ker sent word to the warden that within one week he would burn one of his towns in the centre of his wardenry, and so near to his castle that the blaze would give the Earl light enough to put his clothes on at the hour of midnight.

Knowing the daring character of the Kers, Northumberland placed strong guards upon all the known passes into Scotland; but all too late, for Ker had already crossed far to the north-west and marched to within four miles of Warkworth Castle before a single beacon was lighted. 'Upon Tuesday's night', wrote the Earl to King Henry the Eighth, 'came thirty horsemen into a little village of mine called Whetill having only six houses in it, and there they would have fired the said houses but they forgot to bring fire with them, and so took a wife, being great with child in the town and said to her, where we cannot give the lord light, yet we shall do this in spite of him. They then gave her three mortal wounds in the head, and one in the side with a dagger, whereupon the said wife is dead and the child lost'[1]. While this barbarous murder was being committed the beacon lights were flaming on all the surrounding hills and castles, armed men were closing in and blocking every known line of retreat, and yet, notwithstanding all this, and the immense tract of country over which the marauders had to pass on their return home, they re-crossed the Border without the loss of a single life.

Any attempt to enumerate the raids and fights of this restless period, and yet maintain continuity of narrative, seems hopeless; we have simply a confused and dreary catalogue of burnings, oppression, and slaughter. It is profitable to consider only the

---

[1] Cotton MSS. *Caligula*, Book vi. 24.

larger events, especially those affecting the relationships of the two countries.

The attitude of the two kingdoms during the greater part of the 16th century was bitterly hostile. For a considerable period the hatreds were embittered by the impolitic rule of Cardinal Wolsey, whose ignorance of the peculiar conditions of life on the Border, and Scotch affairs in general, led to many disastrous consequences.

The state of affairs, at last, became so exasperating to King Henry the VIII that he seems to have been lashed into a frenzy, if we may judge from the curious vituperation of his language when he launched against Scotland two of the most savage invasions made since the days of Edward (the Hammer). In the instructions given to the Earl of Hertford, the commander of the army of invasion, he says,

'You are to put all to fire and sword, to burn Edinburgh town and to raze and deface it when you have sacked it and gotten what you can out of it, as that it may remain for ever a perpetual memory of the vengeance of God lighted upon it for their falsehood and disloyalty. Do what you can out of hand and without any tarrying to beat down and overthrow the Castle. Sack Holyrood House, and as many towns and villages about Edinburgh as you conveniently can.

'Sack Leith and burn and subvert it, and all the rest, putting man, woman, and child to fire and sword without exception where any resistance shall be made against you.

'And this done, pass over to the Fife land and extend the extremities and destructions to all towns and villages where into you shall reach conveniently.

'And not forgetting among all the rest to spoil and turn upside down the Cardinal's town of St. Andrews as the uppermost stone may be nether, and not one stick stand by another, sparing no creature alive within the same, especially such as in friendship or blood be allied to the Cardinal'[1].

These instructions, more worthy of an African savage than the zealous defender of the faith of Christ, were carried out by Hertford as far as he was able. Edinburgh and Leith were partly destroyed, the Abbey and Palace of Holyrood were given to the flames, while along the east coast and southward into Teviotdale the country was laid waste, but the devastation not being sufficiently sweeping to satisfy the vengeance of King Henry, a second invasion, under the command of Sir Ralph Eure, was made in the following year (1544).

Eure crossed the Border with a large army and reduced Merse and Teviotdale to ashes, burning the towns of Jedburgh and Kelso, and slaying the inhabitants with great barbarity. One hundred and ninety-two towns and parish churches were destroyed. Ten thousand head of cattle, twelve thousand sheep, two hundred goats, eight hundred and fifty bolls of corn, with an enormous quantity of inside gear, were the fruits of Eure's campaign[2]. Four hundred men were slain and eight hundred taken prisoners. And yet with all this rapine Henry accomplished nothing beyond stirring afresh the fires of hatred smouldering among the Scotch since the Sack of Berwick, and the more recent defeat at Flodden. A policy so entirely remorseless had the effect of binding the Scotch together and putting an end to many of the internal quarrels by which they had been so long weakened as well as alienating from Henry some of those nobles who had been wavering in their loyalty to the Scottish Crown.

King Henry was soon to learn that he had gone a step too far and that a day of reckoning was at hand. He had taken it upon himself to promise to Sir Ralph Eure a grant of all the lands he could conquer

---
[1] Taylor's *History*, vi. p. 583.
[2] Redpath's *Border History*, p. 550.

in Merse, Teviotdale, and Lauderdale. He probably did not know, or had forgotten, that a large portion of these domains belonged to his friend Douglas, Earl of Angus, still residing at his Court in consequence of his strained relations with the Scottish Regent. When Angus heard of the intended transfer of his ancient lands to Eure his indignation knew no bounds. He swore 'that if Ralph Eure dared to act upon King Henry's grant he would write his sasine (or instrument of possession) upon his skin with sharp pens and bloody ink.'

Moved perhaps as much by his personal interests as by his patriotism, Angus promptly put his renowned military skill at the disposal of the Scottish Regent, and with such a force as he could hastily gather together, boldly gave battle to the English army at Melrose. His small and raw force was, however, compelled to retire, but with great skill he kept up continuous assaults upon the English rear, until he was joined by Scott of Buccleuch and Norman Leslie. Thus united, the Scots took up their ground on Ancrum Moor, and prepared for battle. Eure, elated with his many successes looked upon the promiscuous army of the Scots as little better than a rabble to be disposed of by a single charge. Little dreaming that they were so well prepared for the encounter, Eure rushed upon the Scots with headlong fury. A long and fierce battle was fought, in which the Scots were completely victorious. Sir Ralph Eure, instead of entering upon the enjoyment of the domains, lay dead upon the field, along with Sir Brian Layton. A thousand prisoners were taken, among whom were many men of position, from whom considerable sums were exacted as ransom. The defeated English were also attacked by the neighbouring peasantry, notably by the women, who had been rendered furious by the appaling; atrocities of the soldiers of Eure. They joined in the pursuit, calling aloud to 'remember Broomhouse', and one of these Amazons fought with such desperate valour that her heroism has been inscribed upon a stone monument, still to be seen, in the neighbourhood of Ancrum, in the following lines:

> Fair maiden Lilliard lies under this stane,
> Little was her stature, but great was her fame ;
> Upon the English loons she laid many thumps,
> And when they cutted off her legs, she fought upon her stumps.

CHAPTER VI

THE SEVENTH EARL OF NORTHUMBERLAND

THE seventh Earl of Northumberland, English warden of the Eastern and Middle Marches, during the reign of Elizabeth, stands pre-eminent as a man of the highest honour in an age when the nobility in both countries furnished few examples of whom so much could be said.

His father, Sir Thomas Percy, along with many other leading Catholics, had been attainted, and all his worldly possessions confiscated for his share in the Catholic rising historically known as 'the pilgrimage of Grace.' His two sons were left nameless and in poverty,' as by the act of attainder the whole of the vast estates of the Percys passed, after the death of the then holder, to the possession of the Crown. However, the excellent character of the two young men induced the government to permit them to take employment in defence of the Border, so that at an early age they were introduced to all the hardships and excitements of the foray. Thomas, the elder, was a gallant soldier, genial, generous, and popular, but not very capable in the management of affairs. His excellent services on the Border were allowed to pass without reward, or even acknowledgment, throughout the time of King Henry.

After the King's death, however, the Protector Somerset restored both the young men to their mother's lands and to the use of the surname of their race, at the same time conferring upon Thomas the dignity of knighthood. When Mary (a Queen of their own faith) came to the throne she shewed a still higher appreciation of Sir Thomas by raising him to the peerage as Baron Percy of Cockermouth, and soon after creating him Earl of Northumberland, 'in consideration of his descent, constancy, virtue, valour in arms, and other strong qualifications.'

Both the earldom and the barony were to revert, in case of failure of male issue, to his brother Henry and his children, a condition pregnant with extraordinary consequences to the Percy family in the woeful years which followed Queen Mary's death. The earldom and barony were thus created anew, so that, strictly speaking, Sir Thomas was the first Earl of the new creation, rather than the seventh of the creation of the fourteenth century [1].

Besides being raised to all the honours of his family he was restored to the extensive estates in Northumberland, Durham, and Yorkshire, enabling him to take up his residence at Alnwick, the lordly home of his race. Great was the joy of the surrounding inhabitants at seeing the old family once more installed in the historic stronghold of the Percys. We are told that oxen roasted whole were consumed on every village green between Beverley and Berwick, while the beacon fires blazed on the hills far and wide.

The Earl made an almost regal progress through the towns and villages on his southward journey to his beautiful home at Topcliffe, and before the glad congratulations had well subsided the welcome news arrived of the Earl's appointment to the office of Martial of the field against the Scots, to the Lord Wardenship of both the East and Middle Marches, and to the Governorship of Redesdale, Tynedale, and Berwick.

In short, the Earl was beloved by all classes of both religions, and he had devoted friends who remained true to him to the last hour of his sad life.

[1] Nicol, *Synopsis of the Peerage*.

We are told by De-Fontblanque that he was 'singularly affectionate and simple-minded, a warm friend, a jovial and hospitable neighbour. He was a kind and generous master, devoted to field sports and martial exercises, and although of an indolent and irresolute nature, and possessed of little intellectual power, yet by no means devoid of dignity or a due sense of the responsibility attaching to him as the head of his house, and as a great Border chieftain! What faith would have been placed in the prophet who should have foretold that within little more than twelve years this kindly and genial nobleman would have lit the torch of civil war, and passed through penury and exile to an ignominious death upon the scaffold.'

Who could have dreamed when in the spring of 1558 he married and brought home to Topcliffe the accomplished and beautiful Lady Anne Somerset, daughter of William, second Earl of Worcester, said to be the most charming English woman of her day, that so dire a fate was hanging over their happy home?

Immediately upon his appointment as warden, the Earl set vigorously to work to improve the defences along the Border. His great popularity enabled him to unite the services of nearly all the leading men and their retainers, so as to create a powerful force acting together under one command, instead of the old system of each fighting for himself. In this way he was able to station companies of horsemen, each 100 strong, at every pass along the wardenries. And so completely did he check the disorders and raids on both sides of the Border that in a short while a treaty of peace between the two kingdoms was signed in the Church of St Mary at Upsetlington, the Earl of Northumberland and Lord Dacre acting for England, and the Earl of Morton and Lord Dalkeith for Scotland.

The death of Queen Mary at once changed the whole condition of things in the North, where the people, being largely Catholic, had enjoyed special favour during her reign. Under the new Queen (Elizabeth) all Romanists were more or less under suspicion, and clouds began to gather round the head of the great chief, though at first Elizabeth seemed to have kindly inclinations towards him by reason perhaps of the tender associations between a former Percy and her ill-fated mother, Anne Boleyn.

It was the Earl's evil fate, however, to have incurred the deadly aversion of Secretary Cecil, arising partly from jealousy of his extraordinary influence and popularity throughout the North of England, where the success of his rule and the stainless character of his public and private life were a standing rebuke to his own crafty statesmanship, and partly because of the Earl's well-known sympathy with the captive Mary Queen of Scots.

Cecil worked largely by means of spies whom he had in his pay in all ranks and classes, chief among whom was Sir Ralph Sadler, whom he appointed Chancellor of the Duchy of Lancaster with a place on the commission for the defence of the Border, for the express purpose of watching Northumberland closely, and to report the slightest fault or irregularity of which he might be guilty [1].

In time the Earl, finding himself thwarted and checked at every point by Sadler, resigned the wardenship in disgust. Everything was done to lessen the Earl's influence in Northumberland and to influence the mind of Elizabeth against him. Cecil could point to the notorious fact of his warmth in the cause of Queen Mary, and to the strong probability of his being forced, sooner or later, into compromising activity in defence of the faith to which he was devoted. He therefore deemed it the wisest policy to goad Northumberland into some act sufficiently illegal to warrant his arrest before any formidable movement could be organised among his friends and adherents. To attain this end a constant succession

[1] Sadler, *State Papers*, vi. p. 386.

of affronts and injuries were put in practice against him which were endured with exemplary patience, from the Earl's extreme reluctance to take any step which might cast suspicion upon his loyalty to the Crown.

As an example of the singularly mean and malicious methods which Elizabeth's great minister was not ashamed to employ, one may be cited in connection with a copper mine of some value which the Earl was working upon his estate near Newland in Cumberland. Cecil hearing of the considerable revenue derived from this source, determined to lay hands upon it, even in violation of all ancient rights of the owner. By an unprecedented stretch of the Royal prerogative, he succeeded in persuading Queen Elizabeth to seize the whole of the Earl's mineral rights which the Percys had enjoyed since the thirteenth century without challenge. Commissioners were promptly appointed to enter upon and seize the property in the Queen's name. These Commissioners, however, while carrying out Cecil's instructions, seem to have been somewhat shocked at this unheard-of exercise of arbitrary power by an English monarch.

They had the courage and the honesty not only to criticise the iniquity of the deed, but to plead that Lord Northumberland should be allowed some indemnity for the confiscation of his property, particularly considering the large sums spent in the equipment of the works, money spent in the full assurance that he was acting strictly within those laws which protect an Englishman's property, and relying upon the ancient and indefeasible mining rights on a private estate now for the first time overthrown. So reasonable a recommendation as this was unfortunately totally at variance with Cecil's policy of pin-pricks intended to exasperate the Earl into some distinct act of hostility to the Crown in order to precipitate his downfall.

Far from making amends, the original wrong was

aggravated into the most intolerable outrage. Not only was there a denial of compensation, but when Cecil found that the first act of spoliation had been patiently endured, and that there had been no explosion of wrath as he had hoped, a further claim was made against the Earl for the restitution of the ore already extracted and sold; and to crown all, an enormous fine was imposed upon Lord Northumberland for working his own mine without special permission for the Crown [1].

While these scandalous provocations were being heaped upon the Earl, the penal laws against the Catholics of the North were being enforced with such rigour that rumours of a papist rising began to spread, associated more or less with the names of the two prominent Earls of Northumberland and Westmorland. One of the main objects of the disaffected Catholics was the release of Queen Mary of Scotland. Her existence had become a terror to Elizabeth, whose legitimacy had been denied by her own father, thus placing her prisoner, Mary, in the position of rightful heir to the throne of England. This thought, as is so well known, drove Elizabeth almost to madness, and inspired her with a deadly hatred against every friend or sympathiser with the luckless Mary, most of whom were ultimately brought under the axe.

The spies and agents of Cecil supplied him with particulars of all the movements in the North from day to day. Then came news from the President of the North (Lord Sussex), of the existence of a serious conspiracy headed by the two Earls in league with the Duke of Norfolk, the Lords Arundel and Talbot, and many others; their declared object being the release of the Scottish Queen from Tutbury Castle, and the recognition of the Catholic faith.

The receipt of this news, though very alarming to Elizabeth, was by no means unwelcome to Cecil,

[1] Brenan's *House of Percy,* p. 271.

providing, as it did, that long-hoped-for justification for putting in force whatever expedients might be necessary for the final overthrow of his great northern enemy.

As a matter of form the offending Earls were summoned to appear at Court to answer for their conduct. This they wisely declined to do, knowing how often Cecil had courteously invited suspected persons to appear at Court under some plausible promise or other, and then lodged them in the Tower.

This defiance of the Royal summons, as will readily be seen, precipitated the rising long before the plans of the disaffected had reached maturity, precisely as Cecil had cunningly intended it should do.

On hearing that a commission was on its way north to secure their arrest, Northumberland and Westmorland mounted their horses and joined the conspirators who had assembled in some force at Branspeth. After some deliberation, and chiefly influenced by the warlike harangue of Leonard Dacre of Nawarth, and the spirited appeals to their manhood by Lady Westmorland, the meeting resolved upon insurrection.

They were careful however to publish a manifesto declaring their unshaken allegiance to Elizabeth, but their firm determination to re-establish the religion of their ancestors, to remove evil counsellors from the Queen, and to restore the Duke of Norfolk and other faithful peers to their liberty and to the Royal favour[1].

Unlike the fiery Lady Westmorland, Lady Northumberland used all her powers of persuasion to dissuade her husband from taking up the fatal sword of rebellion. She implored him to comply with the Queen's summons, relying for his safety upon the stainless honour of his past life in the service of the State, which could not fail to appeal to the justice of the Queen. To quote her supposed words from the

---

[1] Harleïan MSS., 787 (14), fol. 10.

ancient ballad which so well describes this tragic story :

> Now heaven forfend, my dearest lord,
> That ever harm shall hap to thee ;
> But go to London to the Courte,
> And fair fall truth and honesty.

All her eloquence in favour of patient submission was easily overthrown by the brave words of Dacre and the irrepressible ardour of Lady Westmorland, whose enthusiasm dragged her doubting husband into action perhaps against his better judgment.

Northumberland proposed that the first step in the enterprise should be a descent upon Tutbury Castle for the release of Queen Mary of Scotland.

This would have been easily accomplished, as the castle was known to be feebly garrisoned. Besides, the liberation of the heir to the English throne (herself a reigning Queen) would give importance to the insurrection both in England and Scotland, and would not be unlikely to draw to their standard many sympathisers besides those of their own faith. This seemed altogether too tame a beginning for the impetuous Dacre. Nothing less would serve him than an immediate attack upon the forces under Lord Sussex which had concentrated at Topcliffe Castle, from which place Lord Northumberland had just escaped, and where his ill-starred children yet remained. Before the confused body of insurgents could be drilled into effective military order a most unfortunate circumstance occurred, which threw a serious damper over all their hopes, and, indeed, reduced the whole movement to helpless impotence.

This was the receipt of a most impolitic letter from Pope Pius the Fifth, which the fanatics of the party insisted upon having read aloud to the assembled insurgents, and upon whom it made a profound impression. If the Pope had been content to send them his blessing all would have been well, but when his Holiness proceeded to exhort the insurgents to emulate the example of Saint Thomas à Beckett and to steadfastly refuse to submit to an excommunicated Queen[1] he seemed entirely to have forgotten that the success of the enterprise rested mainly upon powerful Protestant support. This blazing indiscretion of the Holy Father scattered the conspirators to the winds. Had he been a secret agent of Cecil he could not have served his master's will with more deadly effect, for his intervention at that critical moment, with words so hateful to Protestant ears, dissolved the rapidly forming party of the disaffected of both religions as though by a spark of magic. Every one of those Protestant enemies of Cecil, who had joined the rising only to secure his overthrow, now hastened to make their peace.

Well might the northern leaders feel the pangs of mortification when, following hard upon this ill-fated Papal advice, came a letter from the Spanish Ambassador in London urging them to fly for their lives, as all their friends in the South had deserted them, including Lords Derby, Arundel, and Southampton, upon whom they had placed their greatest hopes. So completely lost did the Spanish Ambassador believe their cause, that he had (as a true Catholic) taken it upon himself to make all arrangements to secure their escape into Holland. This, however, the two Earls manfully declined. They would not leave those who had followed them into insurrection face to face with the gathering storm, for well they knew that the wrath of Elizabeth would sweep like a destroying tempest over the north country. There were others among the leaders in the insurgent camp whose fidelity was less highly toned, and when the hour of peril arrived no less a person than their infallible military adviser, the persuasive orator, Leonard Dacre, collapsed at once on hearing the sinister news from the South. His martial spirit deserted him and his eloquence ceased.

[1] Lansdowne MSS.

Quietly he stole away from the council, under the pretence of hunting up recruits, mounted his horse, and fled to Sussex. The Lord President heard his confession, and sent him under guard to London, where, throwing himself at the feet of Elizabeth, and begging for mercy, he betrayed the whole of his companions. His baseness did not end even there, for he actually begged a command in the force under Lord Warwick now leaving London to crush the rebels [1].

The other most notable deserter was Lady Westmorland. On the first signs of failure she cleverly managed to reach a place of safety and made her peace with Cecil, who gladly utilised her valuable evidence, and procured for her a luxurious and comfortable home from the bounty of Elizabeth, which she continued to enjoy all through the many years in which her husband was left to starve in a foreign land.

In spite of all these discouragements the two Earls boldly decided to fight, and having got their ranks in order raised the standard of St Cuthbert.

Their first act of hostility to the Crown of England was an advance upon Durham, where, having seized the cathedral and celebrated mass, they very unwisely burnt the whole of the books of common prayer in one great pile in the cathedral yard. Leaving Durham, they marched to Raby and Bernard Castle, both of which they seized; then in a body 7,000 strong they advanced to Hartlepool, in the hope of being able to put themselves in communication with their sympathisers in the Spanish Netherlands and possibly obtain material help. Meanwhile the great force under Lord Warwick was steadily moving north, and from the reports daily coming to hand the insurgents began to realise how desperate was the task they had undertaken.

Gradually, confusion and panic spread through the

---

[1] Brenan's *House of Percy*.

ranks, which was soon followed by a general dispersion of all the men on foot, flying for their homes in every direction. Five hundred horsemen alone remained, and with these the two Earls rode to Hexham, but being denied admittance the horsemen also dispersed.

All that now remained of the insurgent army were the Earls of Northumberland and Westmorland, Norton of Norton Conyers and his two sons, two Swinbornes, and a few faithful servants. Along with them came one brave heart whose name will be ever memorable on the Borderland: this was Lady Anne, the devoted wife of Lord Northumberland.

Their plight was well-nigh desperate, for they had that remorseless tool of Cecil, Sir John Foster, at the head of one thousand light horse in full pursuit. Sussex, with two thousand more horse and foot, was following fast behind, while the still greater force of Lord Warwick was gradually pushing its way northward. The small band of fugitives had no hope of shelter save among the outlaws of Liddesdale, and in that direction they turned their weary footsteps. There was one house on their way where, if anywhere in England, rest and shelter could not honourably be denied them. This was Nawarth Castle, the home of their recent confederate, Leonard Dacre. The *ci-devant* orator and organiser of the insurrection was now quietly at home in perfect safety among his old oaks, having been pardoned and whitewashed as a reward for his great zeal in betraying his former confederates and dupes. Either the fugitives were as yet ignorant of the full measure of Dacre's baseness, or their condition was so desperate that a short rest and a little food had become imperative.

Be this as it may, they reached Nawarth in a very deplorable condition after the hardships of a week's flight by unfrequented ways over hill and dale. Dacre they found upon his door-step, and begged the favour of his hospitality for a single night—a small favour to ask of one so largely responsible for their sufferings.

Dacre received them with the stony indifference of a stranger; not only did he deny a few hours' rest even to the utterly exhausted Countess, but in his new-born zeal as an agent of Cecil, he had the brazen hardihood to threaten to join the pursuit for their arrest: — conduct eminently characteristic of the false race to which he belonged. Lord Northumberland seems to have been staggered at this unblushing exhibition of baseness. In vain he reminded Dacre of past favours, and appealed to his sense of knightly courtesy to give a little rest and nourishment to the poor lady faint and worn at his door. For surely, said he, if there is one woman on earth entitled to your sympathy, it is the Countess of Northumberland. Such pleadings fell upon deaf ears. Rudely were the fugitives ordered to be gone, for, said Leonard Dacre, 'no rebels shall ever be sheltered in my house.'

Lest worse things might befall them the fugitives felt obliged to press on towards the Scottish Border, receiving, fortunately, many acts of simple kindness from the inhabitants in the villages they passed.

Unlike Dacre of Nawarth, the poor peasants felt their hearts warm to the fallen Earl and his brave wife, once the supreme rulers of the North, and now reduced to beg for shelter among the wild outlaws of Liddesdale.

Late on a cold November night the refugees reached their destination among the wildest and worst of the Armstrong banditti. 'Jock o' the Side', a noted thief, received Lord and Lady Northumberland. 'The laird's Jock' found quarters for Lord Westmorland, and a peculiarly wicked ruffian, known as 'Black Ormiston', arranged for the rest of the party. Ormiston was a Teviotdale Armstrong, the associate and vassal of Bothwell, and known to have assisted in the murder of Darnley.

On the downfall of his lord he had taken refuge in Liddesdale where he found a congenial spirit in 'ill Sim' of Whitehaugh.

Revolting as must have been the society of these outlaws, and coarse their hospitality to people accustomed to the delicacies and the refinements belonging to the exalted station which Northumberland had filled for so many years, still, it was much to find themselves in an acknowledged harbour of refuge, and free from further pursuit. The district called Liddesdale had long been recognised as a sanctuary in which offenders from both countries might deem themselves fairly secure.

Moreover, the Armstrong clan had good reason to respect their old enemy of the Eastern Marches for many an act of clemency, for while Northumberland was warden on the English side, he had always played the Border game right fairly, and many of them knew they owed their lives to his constant observance of 'Liddesdale liberty.' Here the Countess was lodged in a hut with hardly more furniture than the poor bed of bracken upon which she lay, a dwelling afterwards described by Lord Sussex as not to compare with an ordinary dog kennel in England, and here this high-born dame, described as the most brilliant and fascinating woman of her day, settled down bravely to face the rigours and privations of a hard winter.

Meanwhile Cecil's restless energies were devoted to projects for securing the arrest of the fugitives—whose whereabouts he had now discovered — by arrangement with the Lord Regent of Scotland, failing which, he was fully resolved that none of the unwritten laws and customs of Liddesdale should stand between him and the destruction of an enemy so hated, and so full of dangerous possibilities in the uncertain future as Northumberland.

He foolishly began his negotiations with the Regent Moray in a lordly fashion, demanding the immediate expulsion of the rebels from Scottish territory, a demand with which Moray dared not comply even if he had wished. The Regent knew too well the temper of his countrymen, already incensed at the harsh treatment of their Queen; he knew that a wave of the most profound commiseration for the fugitives had moved the hearts of all classes throughout the South of Scotland, and he also knew that the most distinguished of those fugitives was persecuted mainly because of his staunch adherence to the Queen of Scots. The Regent therefore, found himself in a position of extreme perplexity, for well he knew, from past experience, with what dogged persistence Cecil invariably tracked his victims to their doom, however exalted their rank, and what formidable expedients he would unhesitatingly employ rather than be baulked of his prey.

If all negotiations for the surrender of the refugees failed, it was almost certain Cecil would be tempted to invade Liddesdale on his own account; for the destruction of Northumberland had now taken precedence of all else in the minds of both Queen and minister, and nothing would be more certain to raise a storm of uncontrollable resentment in Scotland than a military descent upon the Border for such a purpose. Even the leading Scottish Puritans were loud in their condemnation of the iniquitous oppression which had driven so honourable a man as Northumberland into rebellion, notoriously to effect his ruin, and they were in no temper to submit to threats. But on the other hand the Regent knew that he was not prepared for war with England, and had good reason to dread that the first effect of an adverse conflict would in all probability be his own downfall. There was, however, another alternative by which war might be avoided and the situation turned to profitable account. This was to inveigle Lord Northumberland into Scotland, and if safely lodged in Edinburgh

Castle, not only would an immediate descent upon the Border be checked, but time would be given to negotiate until public interest in the fate of the great prisoner began to subside sufficiently to enable the Regent to deal with Cecil by way of ransom, or rather to sell him for a considerable sum of money.

The difficulty was how to withdraw the Earl from Liddesdale. Any attempt to secure him by force would have been so resented in the South of Scotland as likely enough to precipitate the war Moray was so anxious to avoid. The only method which recommended itself to the Regent was treachery by spies and agents among the outlaws, most of whom were doubtless open to bribes. For this important business the Regent chanced to have in his service one Martin Elliot, a man of Liddesdale origin, who still kept in touch with his friends and relations on the Border, and was in all respects a perfect tool for the purpose.

This creature was at once employed, and duly instructed by the Regent to proceed to Liddesdale on the pretence of a visit to his old home, and while there to worm himself into the confidence of 'Jock o' the Side' and his confederates so as to obtain speech with the two Earls.

This he managed without difficulty, and at once informed them that he was a secret friendly agent sent by the Lord Regent to warn them that danger was impending; that they had information that Cecil, being aware of their exact place of concealment, had already sent a large force which was now rapidly nearing the Border to capture or slay them regardless of Liddesdale customs or ancient rights of sanctuary.

Elliot also played upon the fears and the cupidity of the outlaws, bribing them, and warning them that Cecil would certainly lay waste their country with fire and sword if the fugitives were not at once expelled. The Armstrongs, becoming alarmed, at once joined Elliot in concocting a stratagem by which their dangerous guests might be scared into taking flight without delay. In the dead of night, when all were at rest, the outlaws raised a sudden cry of alarm, calling upon the Earls to fly for their lives, as they pretended to have heard of the rapid approach of the English troops, and soon escape would be impossible. The Earls, having no suspicion of treachery, sprang from their beds, and along with their friends disguised themselves as moss-troopers preparatory to flight. Now, however, they found themselves in a dilemma altogether heart-rending, for the Countess, hitherto so active and brave in all emergencies, was, at this supreme moment, so utterly prostrated by an attack of fever as to make her removal impossible. The continual wear and tear of mind and body, along with wretched food and the damp, unhealthy lodging had at last told upon her delicately nurtured frame. The predicament was appalling, but her courage never wavered for a moment. She insisted upon the immediate flight of the men, and elected with noble courage, ill and helpless as she was, to throw herself upon the mercy of the moss-troopers. If the Earls remained they would be captured and slain, and if they moved the Countess in her fevered condition she would surely die. There was no alternative, therefore, but to bargain with the outlaws for such attentions as they might be induced to bestow, to entreat and implore their kindly consideration, hoping that her sad plight might possibly awaken some little redeeming kindliness in the crime-hardened hearts of Jock o' the Side and his allies. The outlaws promised all that the Earl demanded, and swore they would guard the Countess from all evil. It would be difficult to find a historical parallel for a parting so sad as this between the Earl and Countess of Northumberland in that squalid hut among the thieves of Liddesdale. At their tender leave-taking they knew that every probability pointed towards its being their last farewell, as in point of fact it proved to be. It would be hard to say who was most to be pitied, but one can imagine the poor, sick, desolate wife left alone and likely to die in such an awful place, and how her thoughts, in that dark hour, would revert to the happy days of her early wedded life, to her stately home among the green woods of Topcliffe. What a contrast between that joyous, brilliant past and the woeful present! Wealth, splendour, husband, children, friends, all scattered and gone; nothing left but the ashes of banished illusion!

Jock o' the Side and Black Ormiston accompanied the fugitives some miles on their way towards Canonbie, and, turning, bade them adieu with renewed promises to guard the Countess faithfully.

Perhaps Jock o' the Side may have been sincere in his promise. Not so Black Ormiston, for no sooner had they returned than this unutterable ruffian, regardless of his promise and dead to all sense of pity, broke into the hut where the Countess lay and robbed her of all she possessed, leaving her little save the clothes that covered her.

There is an old saying that when things get to their worst they begin to mend, and so it was with Lady Northumberland; succour was at hand, coming from a quarter where least expected.

I have referred to that marked wave of sympathy with Northumberland and his companions which had rolled along the Border and far into Scotland, touching the hearts of many an ancient foe of the Percy race.

Among those who had heard of the pitiful plight of the Countess in the hands of the outlaws were the ladies of the house of Ferniehirst, a family for years at enmity with the house of Northumberland, and with whom they had crossed swords in many a Border foray. It was characteristic of true Border chivalry that help should come from such a quarter. The warm-hearted ladies of Ferniehirst and their

FERNIEHURST CASTLE: THE TOWER

chivalrous lord rose to the occasion, and determined to rescue the Countess from her loathsome surroundings at whatever cost.

Right gallantly Ker rode off at the head of a well-selected company, on probably the most knightly raid ever heard of on the Borderland.

This raid, without a thought of plunder, prompted by the most sacred instincts of humanity, made its way at great risk to the dangerous district where the Countess lay. Overcoming all difficulties, they found the poor lady, placed her in a specially provided litter, and then, away over moor and moss-hag, the company joyfully bore her along to the friendly welcome awaiting her at Ferniehirst.

On arrival at the castle she was received as an old friend, the ladies Ker surrounding her with all the comforts and attentions their house could afford. With such deeds on record the Border may well boast of its ancient chivalry. At Ferniehirst Lady Northumberland found herself installed as an honoured guest in the very centre of the hereditary foes of her husband's house. All feuds and animosities were put aside, and every head bowed in respect and admiration for this noble woman's great heart which could grapple with such conditions and endure such horrors for the sake of her beloved lord.

In addition to the kindly welcome from the Kers, the Countess had soon the gratification of knowing that all the great Border houses had enthusiastically embraced her cause. Among the first who came to offer help was the Lord Home, a leading Puritan and a great chief. Scott of Buccleuch and many others assured her of their determination to make any sacrifice to protect her husband from the vengeance of Queen Elizabeth and Cecil.

CHAPTER VII

NORTHUMBERLAND BETRAYED

On the highway between Canonbie Church and Newcastleton—a short distance beyond Rowanburn village—may be seen the gable end of a small farm-house, perched high on the hillside to the left on the way north. This farm is interesting, as having been built on the site of the old stronghold of Hector Armstrong, known to history as Hector the traitor of Harelaw. It was to this stronghold that Northumberland and his fugitives made their way on parting from Jock o' the Side and Black Ormiston. They had a double inducement in turning their steps in that direction. In the first place, it was within the debateable land, and immune from invasion, not merely by time-honoured right of sanctuary as in Liddesdale, but by actual treaty between the two countries. And, in the second place, this Harelaw was the strong tower of Hector a raider, well known in Northumberland, and one upon whose hospitality the Earl had peculiar claims.

It chanced that when Northumberland was Lord Warden of the English Marches Hector had been obliged to fly into England, pursued by 'hot trod, hue and cry', when his life was saved by his falling into the hands of the too considerate Earl. Northumberland not only sheltered, but housed, him for a long period, and when the storm, caused by his misdeeds, had subsided, helped him to return to Canonbie in safety. Northumberland, from the natural instincts of his own noble mind, had never a doubt but that the reiver's gratitude for so great a service rendered in his desperate struggle for life could now be confidently relied upon when the tables were turned and his own life was in danger.

Hector pretended to be glad to meet Northumberland and his friends, and readily promised to maintain strict secrecy as to his place of concealment, and to aid him and his companions in every way. Under the supervision of honest Hector a cunning hiding-place was found in a cave known only to himself, and so situated that he could readily warn the refugees of approaching danger. Here they pitched their camp, in the fullest confidence that their guard or sentinel, bound by the strongest ties of gratitude, was above suspicion. All seemed to go well for a time, until the reappearance of the clever Martin Elliot upon the scene aroused their anxieties. The Regent Moray had been well pleased with the successful stratagem by which Elliot had withdrawn the fugitives from Jock o' the Side and his comrades, and had now instructed him in the plans to be adopted for the capture of the one supremely desired prize, Lord Northumberland; Lord Westmorland and the others being of secondary consideration.

As an open raid could not be made into the debateable land without violation of the treaty, and without raising the whole countryside in angry opposition, it became necessary to proceed with extreme caution, and, by the free use of treachery and bribes, to pounce upon the Earl at some unguarded moment when separated from his friends. Elliot seems to have had little difficulty in making his bargain with the grateful Hector, who as readily agreed to sell his noble benefactor for so much good cash down as he would a herd of stolen nolt. When the price had been settled to his satisfaction the plausible traitor paid a visit to the camp of the unhappy man, on the pretence of having some important news to communicate, intended for Northumberland alone, whom he respectfully desired to walk along with him a little way. Suspecting no harm, the Earl rose and readily accompanied Hector, listening to his talk, unthinkingly moving onward and still onward in the direction of the fatal trap which was prepared and waiting to clutch him. As they neared the appointed spot Martin Elliot joined them, and engaged Northumberland in conversation, in order that Hector might fall behind and give the signal to the party in ambush. Speedily a body of light horsemen galloped out from behind the hill, closed round them, and the great Earl was at last a prisoner at the disposal of the Scottish Regent.

The noise of the arrest having reached their ears, Westmorland and his friends were soon in their saddles and tearing along in full chase! Few as they were, they gallantly rode until they overtook the escort near Langholm. They charged them with such desperate fury that Captain John Borthwick, the leader of the company, paid for his share in the foul business with his life. Outnumbered as they were, however, the rescue was impossible. The Earl was borne along to Hawick, then to Jedburgh, and finally secured within the walls of Edinburgh Castle[1].

While these events were going on the leading Border families were using every effort to induce the Regent to make common cause with the fugitives in open defiance of Elizabeth and Cecil. Lord Home not only invited the Countess to take up her permanent residence at Home Castle, but, hearing from her that Westmorland, Norton, and others were still in hiding in Canonbie, he sent a friendly escort to bring them thither to join her as his guests.

These marked attentions to the refugees, especially to the Countess, being reported to Cecil by Sir Ralph Sadler, a warning was sent to Home that his gallantry was likely to lose him the favour of the great minister.

---

[1] 'Diurnal of Remarkable Occurrents', published in the *Transactions of the Bannatyne Club*, 1833.

To this Lord Home replied that he would sooner give his head than do so foul a deed as betray either the Countess or her lord. The conduct of the Regent throughout was dark and deceitful. To please the powerful sympathising lords, whose support he feared to alienate, he pretended at times to be altogether in favour of espousing the cause of the fugitives, all the while he was secretly negotiating with Cecil in regard to their ultimate fate. In Cecil's own words, 'Moray was found to be in good readiness to chase them to their ruin.'

Moray had now good reason to act with great caution, for other causes of resentment against Elizabeth were beginning to assume formidable proportions not unlikely to lead to hostilities; mainly her harsh and unwomanly treatment of her prisoner, Mary of Scotland, added to the merciless vengeance she was now inflicting upon the disarmed and helpless insurgents in Tynedale and Redesdale, especially the friends and tenants of Northumberland. Sir George Bowes boasted that in less than a fortnight he had put to death about 600 suspected rebels, for, said he, 'the best fruite a tree can bear is a dead traytour[1]'. Among the peasantry, and those unable to escape the gallows by dint of bribery, the slaughter was enormous.

The Queen, over her own signature, absolutely forbade any of the ordinary forms of justice, complaining that quite enough valuable time was wasted in the hanging of a papist without allowing him the benefit of a trial[2]. In all more than 2000 persons are said to have perished, and yet the Queen's thirst for blood was only whetted, for we find her writing to Sussex as follows: 'We marvel that we have heard of no executions by martial law, as was appointed of the meaner sort of rebels of the North. If the same be not already done, you are to proceed

---

[1] Sharp, *Memorials*, p. 153.
[2] Brenan's *House of Percy*, p. 318.

thereunto for the terror of others with expedition'. Under all these circumstances the Regent saw that his policy of evasion and quibbling must be abandoned, and there was now no alternative but to brave the anger of Cecil by a definite refusal to surrender his captive. There was therefore no course open to Elizabeth but a warlike demonstration against the Border of such magnitude as would alarm the proud Scots, and frighten Moray into submission.

A spy called Constable, a former friend of Lord Westmorland, had been sent to hang about Home Castle as a friendly visitor, but really to watch the movements of the fugitives living there, and from him Cecil heard of the determined opposition of all classes in Scotland against the surrender of Lord Northumberland. Constable further related in his report how bitter was the indignation expressed on all sides against the traitor Hector of Harelaw for having betrayed his benefactor. While resting in an inn he had listened to the most scathing denunciations of the villain, the speakers declaring they would like to eat his head for supper. 'To take Hector's cloak' had become a proverb on the Border for the betrayal of a friend. Sir Ralph Sadler also wrote to the Lord Admiral saying that 'the Earl was in the custody of the Regent, and the Countess of Northumberland, the Earl of Westmorland and others were received, aided, and maintained against the Regent's will by the Lord Home, the Lord of Ferniehirst, the Lady of Buccleuch, and others.'

A large force under the command of Sir Henry Gates was sent to threaten the Border with destruction, and when this formidable armament reached the north, Gates forwarded an ultimatum to the Regent, demanding in insolent terms the immediate surrender of all the English insurgents harbouring in Scotland. The Regent, now seriously alarmed, assumed a more temporising attitude, and begged for time. In constant dread of the hot temper of his countrymen he began to conduct a series of complicated and dangerous negotiations without the slightest reference to his Council.

The final outcome of these secret dealings with the crafty Cecil was the conclusion of a memorable bargain fraught with great possibilities, but doomed to remain a dead letter, by reason of a tragic event which took the country by surprise. This bargain was no less than an agreement for the exchange of prisoners. Moray had enlarged upon the ill-treatment of Queen Mary, still detained captive in England against the wishes of her subjects, and suggested that to exchange her for Northumberland would be a complete solution of all difficulties. It is not believed that there was the slightest sincerity in the proposal, which was merely made to gain time, as Moray and all the world believed that Elizabeth's deadly fangs upon her cousin, the *legitimate* heir to her throne, would never be relaxed at any price. It is little wonder, therefore, that the Regent was staggered when Elizabeth expressed her willingness to agree to the proposed exchange. He was not prepared for this, and had good reason to tremble at the great responsibility he had assumed in carrying forward a transaction of such transcendant importance to the kingdom without the knowledge or advice of any single member of the Council. Again he begged time for further consideration, but Lord Hunsdon, the English minister in Scotland, having pressed him to sign the treaty which was to give freedom to Queen Mary, and the headsman's axe to Northumberland, he was obliged to summon the Council to assemble at Linlithgow in order to procure its ratification. Whether the Council would have done so will never be known, for when it assembled no Regent came to preside over it. Instead of sending Northumberland to his doom, he himself lay stark and stiff, slain by the hand of an assassin.

With the death of the Regent Moray the proposed

exchange of prisoners fell to the ground, but the Scottish partisans of the refugees swelled in numbers, and as news came to hand of the wholesale massacres and confiscations of the suspected rebels, the heat increased to such a degree that Scott of Buccleuch and Ker of Ferniehirst organised a raid upon a great scale in defence of the oppressed. Along with them rode the Earl of Westmorland, who had the satisfaction of seeing the forces of Elizabeth attacked, defeated, and scattered by his bold Border protectors. Immense quantities of goods and cattle, taken from the Northumbrian Catholics, were recaptured after desperate fighting in spite of the numerical superiority of the English troops. This successful raid determined Elizabeth to strike at the Scots with her whole might. For a time the persecuted rebels were left alone in order that she might concentrate the whole of her military resources upon a great invasion of Scotland. A vast army was collected, which crossed the Border in three divisions. Sussex advanced through Northumberland. Sir John Forster and Lord Scrope came from the Middle and West Marches respectively.

An attack was made upon Home Castle, but no refugees were found there. Ferniehirst was taken and plundered, 500 villages and 50 castles were, according to Sussex, given to the flames (a wild exaggeration), but the hiding-place of the fugitives remains a secret to this day.

Long before the English had even crossed the Border, the new Regent, the Earl of Mar, had removed the Earl of Northumberland to Lochleven Castle, where he occupied the rooms so recently used as the prison of Mary Queen of Scots. The great invasion proved a dismal failure, and gradually degenerated into useless and indiscriminate raiding, in which there were hard knocks on both sides, until it finally fizzled out without the capture of a single fugitive.

LINLITHGOW PALACE

When the storm of war had blown over, the Countess again came forth from her place of concealment and resumed her efforts in the interest of her husband, hoping to escape with him to Holland. Unfortunately, she soon discovered that his Scotch custodians had become more keenly alive than ever to the value of their prize, and that no freedom could be hoped for without the payment of an immense ransom.

The keeper of Lochleven, responsible for the Earl's safety, was William Douglas, a tool of the Regent, and the official to whom the Countess was obliged to appeal. Both the Regent and Douglas had a keen eye to the main chance, and believing that an enormous ransom could be exacted from the Earl's rich relations, they were resolved to squeeze out of them the last farthing.

It will be observed with some wonder that these men at the head of affairs in Scotland seem to have felt no shame in dealing with a broken-hearted woman piteously pleading for her husband's life with all the remorseless rapacity and juggling which one associates with the lowest type of Greek brigands. After long and wearisome haggling the sum of 10,000 crowns (£2000) was definitely fixed as the lowest price Douglas would entertain for the freedom of Northumberland, but on application to the wealthy kindred, the Countess found that not one of them would, or dared, assist her lest they should compromise themselves with the all-powerful minister. In vain she appealed to many who had fed upon her husband's bounty, rising to wealth and importance by his help in the days of his great wardenship. No one would run the risk of helping the escape of one whose blood Elizabeth had offered to purchase even at the enormous price of Queen Mary's freedom.

Disappointed though she was, her courage was unabated. She would leave no stone unturned so long as life lasted, and now she resolved upon going to the Continent and begging for help in Rome or the Spanish Netherlands. Knowing, however, the slippery character of the knaves with whom she had to deal, she was careful before going to have a written agreement with Douglas of Lochleven in regard to all the conditions of the bargain and the exact price to be paid to him for her lord's life.

When her arrangements were completed she started her journey under the friendly protection of Lord Seaton, accompanied by Lord Westmorland and others of the fugitive party. On their way to Old Aberdeen, the intended port of embarkation, they had to pass Lochleven Castle, but it is not known whether the Countess was allowed a word of farewell, if so, it was the last in this world.

If any further proof were wanted of the dauntless spirit of this noble woman it is to be found in the fact that in these last days of physical strain and mental torture she was so near her confinement that the party had to wait at Old Aberdeen until after the birth of a daughter, the Lady Maria 'the child of sorrow', as her mother called her, who proved to be the comfort and solace of the last years of her life [1].

It seems strange that, notwithstanding the long delay at Aberdeen at a time when spies and agents were swarming along the eastern coast, the escape of the fugitives was unknown to the English government until they were reported to have arrived in Antwerp. This port they reached absolutely penniless, their small purse having been exhausted by the unexpected delay in Old Aberdeen, and their clothes were almost in rags. By this time, however, the story of their wrongs and persecution had travelled all over Europe, and friendly assistance flowed in to the Countess from many quarters.

Within a few weeks of their arrival in Antwerp 4000 crowns were subscribed towards the Earl's

[1] Brenan's *House of Percy*.

ransom from people of means living in the Netherlands, and, to crown all, the full amount of the Douglas ransom was covered by a gift of 6000 crowns from Philip of Spain. This was a triumph indeed, sufficient to fill the heart of the Countess with joy and thankfulness. The door of escape seemed at last to be opened, and soon her beloved one would be far beyond the reach of Cecil's vengeance.

Her bright hopes were soon again over-clouded, new difficulties were raised, Douglas showed a surly reluctance to fulfil his bargain. He would not release the Earl until the actual gold coin was paid down to him. This the agents of Philip were willing to do if Douglas would give them a written guarantee that he would faithfully perform the conditions of his bargain with Lady Northumberland, but no such guarantee would he give. Great efforts were made, but Douglas declined to yield. On the other hand, the Spanish agent, fearing the rogue intended to collar the ransom and cheat the Countess by some suddenly discovered reason for the Earl's continued captivity, declined to trust him. Great haggling went on for a long time without result, Lady Northumberland labouring with all her might to bring the parties to agreement. The letters of appeal she wrote to Douglas few men, having the ordinary instincts which belong to human nature, could have resisted [1]. She pledged her own personal faith that the money should be paid to the last farthing, and implored him to display that knightly courtesy and generous spirit which had ever prevailed between the houses of Douglas and Percy, and even offered herself as a hostage in Northumberland's stead [2]. She appealed to Morton, the head of the house of Douglas and future Regent of Scotland, to use his influence with her husband's gaoler, but all to no purpose. To nothing less than the payment of the 10,000 crowns down, without

---

[1] *Murdin*, p. 186.
[2] Brenan's *House of Percy*, p. 328.

more than a verbal promise to release the Earl, would Douglas agree.

No thought of saving a brave and honourable man from the scaffold, or the heart-breaking entreaties of his devoted wife, in any way disturbed the keen calculations of profit which occupied the close attention of Douglas.

CHAPTER VIII

THE COUNTESS BETRAYED

DURING the time that these fruitless negotiations were on foot the poor Countess had again the evil fortune to fall into the toils of a traitor called John Lee, who had wormed himself into the confidence of Lord Westmorland under the pretence of being an exile like himself, but all the while a spy in the pay of Cecil.

Through this wretch Cecil was regularly informed of all the dealings in progress between the Countess and Douglas of Lochleven. Copies of all the correspondence regarding the raising and paying of the ransom were sent, from which Cecil saw that, after all his fruitless raids and bluster, the question of the Earl's surrender was merely the payment of a moderate amount of cash.

He determined therefore at once to outbid the Countess for her lord, and with this intent he instructed Lord Hunsdon, the Ambassador in Scotland, to sound Douglas upon the point. Hunsdon found Douglas quite ready to nibble at the bait, but for some reason or other he shied at the hook.

In point of fact he was not free to deal without consultation with his partners, one of whom was the Earl of Morton, and the other the Lord Regent himself. These three statesmen, thinking the line of greatest safety to themselves lay in dealing with Cecil rather than the Countess, agreed to accept from

Hunsdon the exact sum which had been raised by her so bravely and laboriously.

But now, when the question of payment arose, all the former difficulty presented itself which had ruined the efforts of the Countess. Morton's agents demanded not only that the gold should be paid down in advance, but in order to screen himself from public resentment he also required a formal demand for Northumberland's surrender, suggesting that it should be made on the plea of treaty obligations [1]. To this Cecil would not agree, and a long period of angry disputation ensued, accompanied with threats of another invasion, and no settlement was reached until the end of May, 1572. Finally it was agreed that the gold should be counted down before the accredited representative of the Regent, and handed over to him the moment Lord Northumberland was securely in custody in England.

And so at last Cecil was triumphant, the Countess crushed, and the Earl brought within the clutches of Elizabeth, who knew no mercy.

All knowledge of this foul treachery had been carefully concealed from Northumberland, who met his keeper daily in friendly intercourse. Douglas always referred to him as 'our honoured guest' with many assurances of sympathy and regard. These friendly protestations were intended to facilitate the Earl's removal, which could only be safely done by some skilful stratagem in which the Earl would appear to be acting voluntarily. Douglas was aware that if the actual facts of the surrender oozed out in the then temper of the Scots there would in all probability be a popular tumult and an effort at rescue. Any attempt to cross the Border, which was still seething with indignation at the Harelaw treachery, would have been so highly hazardous that a plan was contrived by which the prisoner should be sent by sea. The danger, however, of crossing the country to the nearest seaport, with the Earl a

[1] Brenan's *History, House of Percy*, vi. p. 336.

prisoner under guard, was to be avoided by having recourse to a singularly base trick which easily imposed upon the honest and simple-minded lord.

Lord Northumberland, being passionately fond of sport, had made the acquaintance of a neighbouring squire called Cleish, with whom he had occasionally been allowed to spend a day in the fields, with the result that a considerable intimacy sprang up between them. This Cleish, then, was the instrument employed to entice the Earl into joining a fishing expedition to the Bass Rock, where the sport was said to be abundant. Lord Northumberland embraced the opportunity with delight, and Douglas, after making a cunning show of resistance, and Cleish taking upon himself the full responsibility of conducting the Earl safely home again, the party, accompanied by a few boatmen and servants, joyously made their way to the nearest port on the Firth of Forth. Thence they sailed down the Firth, but whether they indulged in any sport is not recorded. Probably Cleish, with the deadly secret in his heart, had lost his relish for such innocent enjoyment. Soon the Earl realised the dastardly trap into which he had been ensnared, for under Cleish's orders the boatmen were directed to make all haste for the port of Dunbar. On their arrival there the Earl found all arrangements had been made for his reception. A considerable company of soldiers, under the command of Sir John Forster, was waiting to receive him, and when he stepped ashore he was at once seized and carried to a place of temporary confinement. The news of his surrender spread rapidly, and crowds began to assemble, angry shouts were heard on all sides, necessitating an immediate removal to Berwick.

But Berwick was also boiling with resentment, for the whole country around this town was devoted to the house of Percy, and to prevent a rescue it became necessary to call in an overpowering military force.

Sir Herbert Maxwell, in his interesting history of

the house of Douglas, refers to this great stain upon their race in the following scathing terms:

'What made his (Douglas of Lochleven) conduct in this affair peculiarly execrable was that he encouraged the unfortunate Countess to bid up to the sum fixed for the Earl's ransom (10,000 crowns), and then when she wrote from Mechlin to say that she had managed at last, and after great difficulty, to scrape the money together, and sent the directions for her husband's journey to rejoin her, Douglas took exactly that sum from Sir John Forster in exchange for his prisoner who was taken to York and there beheaded.'

The shame of this foul transaction has generally been laid more upon the Earl of Morton than even upon his Lochleven kinsman, by way of justifying the numerous charges of avarice made against him.

Some have tried to exonerate him altogether from any share in the transaction on the ground that he had originally protested to Moray, the late Regent, against the arrest of Northumberland in Canonbie, which he then denounced as a shame and reproach, and a violation of the Border customs to succour banished men [1].

Queen Elizabeth was greatly jubilant on hearing that the Earl was now in her hands, and promptly signed a warrant for his execution without thinking it necessary to consult her minister.

When Cecil informed her, however, that the immediate gratification of her thirst for vengeance would entail a substantial loss to her revenue she received a check she had not anticipated. She failed to understand that the whole of the large revenues from the Northumberland estates, which the Crown had seized and enjoyed from the moment of the Earl's outlawry, would pass at his death to his brother, Sir Henry Percy, in accordance with the patents of the late Queen Mary, the attainder and execution of the

[1] Hunsdon to Cecil, Jan. 11th, 1571.

Earl in no way affecting the succession of the said brother.

The predicament was one of the most extraordinary in English history, a conflict between vengeance and avarice, but not an insuperable conflict in the hands of so crafty a minister as Cecil. In a marvellously short space of time he was able to plant his traps so cunningly that the simple-minded country gentleman, Sir Henry Percy, found himself involved in a quarrel with the government.

He was arrested upon various trumped-up charges and lodged in the Tower. The much-required attainder soon followed, leaving Elizabeth in free possession of the Northumberland revenues and the obstacle removed between her and her victim.

A new warrant was placed in the hands of Sir John Forster (who had now moved his prisoner to Alnwick Castle), with orders to proceed to York and there have the Earl beheaded. So restless was the state of the country and so numerous were the demonstrations of sympathy with the Earl, that the intended execution was kept a dead secret. In order to make the journey to York in safety, Forster gave it out that the Earl had at last made his peace with the Queen, and was now travelling to London to be reinstated in all his titles and possessions; but care was taken to have Northumberland surrounded by a large force of picked men.

On their way great numbers of people, including most of the gentry, joined the cavalcade, and when the party reached York they found the streets thronged with a multitude of excited people.

Forster, seeing from the menacing attitude of the inhabitants that no time was to be lost, informed the Earl that he must prepare for death within twenty-four hours. He was not allowed to see a priest of his own faith, nor even to write a last farewell to his beloved wife. He refused to take any rest, but spent the night in prayer and fasting, all the while pestered with the attentions of a Puritan preacher who had been allowed to intrude upon his last sad hours, to warn him of the danger to his immortal soul of dying an obstinate Papist.

Doubtless his last troubled, bewildered thoughts would be fixed upon her who had been the light of his life. The sense of her presence may have for a moment gladdened him in that strange and fantastic dreamland on the confines of the kingdom of eternity.

When the axe fell we are told there was a great groan and burst of weeping from the assembled spectators. Those of his own faith, regarding him as a blessed martyr, gathered up his blood with their handkerchiefs and carried it away as a sacred relic.

Northumberland's stainless character in an age of corruption, his wise and just rule as Lord Warden in the tempestuous reiver-ridden country which he tamed, and his boundless generosity, endeared him to the hearts of all good men from Berwick to the Humber, irrespective of either politics or creed.

It only remains to be stated that his decapitated head was stuck upon a pole, high over the Micklegate Bar, where it remained two years, a hideous reminder of the unwomanly savagery of the 'good Queen Bess', and the craft and duplicity of Cecil, the great Lord Burleigh.

It is interesting to know that the division of the ransom led to an unseemly brawl among the various partners. Cleish, who so cleverly landed the prisoner at Dunbar, considered his manly achievement deserving a greater share of the plunder than the others would allow. Douglas of Lochleven claimed a full thousand pounds, declaring he had spent quite that in giving entertainments to the Earl.

Neither Mar nor Morton were content, and the wrangling continued until, we are told, they came to blows. It is remarkable, too, that nearly all those concerned in this black business came to a miserable end. Mar died within the year, of poison it was said, given at the instance of Morton, who himself perished on the scaffold a few years later.

The brave and devoted wife was now finally overthrown, stricken to the heart by this last terrible trial of pitiless destiny. For a time she was crushed, prostrated, and silent. Apparently she had disappeared from the world, to be heard of no more. Honours and rewards were bestowed upon her enemies and persecutors, and in this connection, perhaps, no more eloquent commentary upon Cecil's evil policy could be produced than the fact that he urged the Regent Moray to grant a free pardon to the outlawed ruffian, Black Ormiston, as a reward *for his service to the Queen*[1] in his treatment of the Countess.

There soon came a time, however, when the dauntless Countess cast aside her unavailing woe and sprang once more upon the world's stage a completely changed individual. The patient pleading, long-suffering woman seemed suddenly transformed into an imperious, resolute Queen, burning with hatred against Elizabeth and Cecil, upon whom she poured her scorn and detestation.

Eagerly she sought out every means of wreaking her vengeance against them both at whatever cost. She wrote a scathing attack upon the government, exposing the long series of iniquities practised by Cecil, with the Queen's concurrence, and always for Elizabeth's personal profit and advantage, even at the cost of confiscation and death to many of the noblest in the land. Her friends warned and begged her in vain to be silent, for never before had any subject dared to use such outspoken language in criticism of Elizabeth. She had her clever pamphlet published in Liége and circulated far and wide, not

[1] Sharpe, *Memorials*.

only in England, but throughout the Continent. It contained every detail of the scandalous seizure of the copper mine and the many deliberately planned acts of oppression by which a high-minded and patriotic peer was driven to rebellion, plundered to feed the avarice of the Queen, and then deprived of his life. The most minute details of the schemes and trickery employed to incriminate the heir in order to extend the attainder to him also, so that Elizabeth might continue in the enjoyment of the Percy revenues after she had slain the head of the house, were set forth in language so clear and stirring that Cecil was staggered and alarmed. Elizabeth was driven into a state of anger similar to the wild frenzies of her father, King Henry, at the bold charges made against her which she could neither deny nor meet with customary punishment.

Cecil was compelled to publish a reply which, though lengthy, took no note of the chief charges against him. The incident of the copper mine he entirely ignored; indeed, the weakness of his reply so strengthened the case against him, that the Countess received it with triumph, had it translated into French, and published along with her own in one volume. The scorn and contempt with which both Queen and Minister were discussed drove them to a useless and impotent fury, for the Countess remained far beyond the reach of their vengeance, dying in exile at Namur in 1591.

The indignation felt along the Border at the deplorable fate of the Earl of Northumberland was productive of many pithy ballads, some of which are quoted by Bishop Percy in his *Reliques*. One of the most notable says:

> Fy on thee, Scotland, and thy seed,
>   Above all realms, woe thee befall,
> Thy lords have done so shameful deed
>   That traitors ay men will you call.
> You are so greedy on English gold
> That all your credit now is sold.

Another, to be found in the Cotton manuscripts in the British Museum, says:

> Who shall hereafter trust a Scot?
> Or who will do that nation good
> That do themselves so stain and blot
> In selling of such noble blood?
> Let lords by this a mirror make,
> And in distress that land forsake.

It is to be observed, however, that the guilt of the Earl's betrayal was fairly divided between a set of unprincipled villains belonging quite as much to the English as to the Scottish side of the Border.

CHAPTER IX

EXTENSIVE REIVING

THE merciless character of the invasions of Scotland during the reign of King Henry the Eighth, and the long continued hostility between the two kingdoms in the time of Elizabeth, had produced, as we have seen, conditions of implacable hatred on both sides of the Border. During the six years, from 1581 to 1587, raiding was incessant, and was indeed the chief occupation of the inhabitants of every class.

Nearly all the movable property in the district was more or less afloat on the wings of the foray, cattle, corn, and goods in general, being tossed about among the raiders until all trace of original ownership was hopelessly lost. Such a time of fighting and pillaging, denouncing and hanging had not been known since the stormy outburst provoked by the massacre of Berwick. Indeed there had been little progress in the methods of civilisation between Berwick and the Solway since the days of Johnie of Gilnockie half a century earlier.

Among the multitude of cases which came before the Warden's Court at this tempestuous period we have some of special interest, both from the importance of the chiefs involved in the raids, and the extraordinary value of the property stolen.

From all the records we have it seems beyond doubt that the Armstrongs of Whitehaugh and Mangerton were the chief offenders on the Scottish side, while the immense clan of the Grahams of

Eskdale gave a pretty good—or bad—account of themselves on the Cumbrian Borders. Some of the worst of these cases were purely acts of vengeance.

Simon Musgrave brings a charge against the laird of Whitehaugh and his accomplices for burning his barns containing wheat, rye, oats, and peas to the value of £1000, but makes no claim for stolen goods. On the same occasion, however, the laird is further accused by the widow of Martin Taylor, of having raided her home, slain her husband, and three of his servants, and carried away 140 of her cattle, and 100 sheep valued at £200. They are also charged with having slain John and William Tweedel, and one David Bell, at the same time capturing ten prisoners to be held to ransom, and lifting 100 cattle, horses, writings and money to the value of four hundred pounds sterling.

Sir Thomas Musgrave and Tom of Todhill charge Robert and Simon Elliot of Park in Liddesdale, along with their accomplice, 'Clemie' Crozier, with stealing 60 cattle, and taking Tom Routledge prisoner.

Walter Scott, lord of Buccleuch, is accused by Thomas Musgrave, the deputy of Bewcastle, with stealing 200 of his cattle, and 300 of his sheep.

In nearly all these cases there are cross claims and hard swearing on both sides; indeed the laird of Mangerton poses as a very ill-used gentleman, for he charges John and Cuddy Taylor not only with a wholesale theft of his cattle and goods valued at £1500, but also with taking him prisoner. Then to add to his *unmerited* misfortunes, Adam and James Forster, with their thievish allies swept down upon his lands at Tweeden, robbing him of 800 sheep and 300 cattle.

But the losses of Mangerton sink into insignificance beside the grievances which his friend, the laird of Whitehaugh, brings before the Warden's Court, from which it would appear that these Taylors from Cumberland could hold their own right sturdily against the terrible men of Liddesdale[1]. According to Whitehaugh, the Taylors had robbed him of silver, coined and uncoined, to the value of four thousand pounds sterling. It would be interesting to know by what honest means Armstrong became possessed of this great wealth in silver while living among the bare hills of Liddesdale.

Robert Elliot of Redheugh (ancestor of the families of Stobs and Minto) accuses Richard Graham of the Mote, and Thomas Carlton, of stealing 60 head of cattle, and carrying away three prisoners for ransom; while Walter Scott of Buccleuch, and the tenants of Ettrick, charge Will Graham of Rose Trees, and Hutchin Graham of Gards, with stealing 120 cattle and 160 sheep. This last case is interesting from the fact that Buccleuch, the complainant, and Hutchin Graham, the accused, became close allies about this time, and acting together, broke into Carlisle Castle in order to rescue their friend, Kinmont Willie, a romantic exploit which will be briefly described in a later chapter.

From the numerous accusations against the Grahams of Mote and Netherby we gather that their raids at this period into the country of their ancestors were upon a truly lordly scale. The value of their plunder is put down at a figure so enormous that some better evidence than that of aggrieved reivers would be needed to convince one of its accuracy.

We find Walter Graham of Netherby and Rob of the Fauld charged by Robert Maxwell of Castlemilk, in Dumfriesshire, with stealing cattle from him to the value of 4000 merks Scotch, while Lord Maxwell (himself a raider of great fame) accuses these worthies of lifting live stock belonging to him to the value of five hundred pounds sterling.

But the most serious charge against the Grahams comes from 'the friends' of Adam Carlyle and the Bells of Dumfriesshire, who accuse them of burning

[1] *Border History.*

Goddesbrigg and lifting three thousand cattle, four thousand sheep and five hundred horses, the whole damage being estimated at forty thousand pounds Scotch, and apparently in the same great raid they were accused of burning Tinwald, Rawchamer, and Micklewoodside, and clearing these townships of 800 cattle and 60 horses, the whole loss being valued at ten thousand pounds.

A further complaint is made against the Grahams of Mote and Netherby by the Scottish Warden of the Western Marches for 'bigging' houses, pasturing cattle and growing corn in Scotland for the past ten years, for which a large indemnity is claimed [1].

It seems extremely probable that the wildest exaggeration prevailed in estimating claims in order to secure some advantage in the ultimate compromise which was frequently the only solution in settling questions of raid and counter raid. Besides, in all these trials before the Warden's Court both accusers and accused were well aware that the decision of the Court was influenced by the power and position of the litigants, and scarcely at all by the impartial consideration of proved facts. Such trials partook more of the character of stormy disputes between English and Scotch men in which the judges themselves, as we have seen, were at times personally interested in the profits of the raid, the criminality of which they had assembled to investigate and punish. The only explanation which can be given for the long-continued endurance of this travesty of justice, even by sixteenth century raiders, is that they were all more or less conscious that the measure of iniquity amongst them was pretty evenly balanced, and when conviction and punishment fell upon the least guilty it might arouse their pity but not their protests. When all were conscious of transgressions for which they had luckily not been called to account, they

[1] *Border History.*

made no great objection to the application of the rope to the wrong man now and then.

Such men are not to be judged by our modern standards of rectitude in public and private affairs. The principle of doing to others as you would be done by would have sounded a comical doctrine in the ears of men like ill Sim of Whitehaugh, accustomed as he and his forefathers had ever been to execute justice and to maintain their own ideas of truth in their own fine old convincing Border fashion, at the head of a well-equipped troop of horse. The trials before the wardens had their comic as well as their tragic side which at times must have tickled the public sense of humour. The earnest attitude of respectability assumed by the most notorious thieves and their loudly expressed abhorrence of cattle lifting must have been delightfully interesting to their confederates. The raider's story of his wrongs was always so sad and so plausible as to lead one to believe that he was a deeply injured innocent. But alas, when the actual facts came under review, of his slaughterings, burnings, and thievings, it was enough to make one's hair stand on end.

According to his own story the Scotch reiver was a quiet, well-disposed, industrious person wanting nothing so much as to be left alone in pursuit of his honest occupations, but whose life was made a burden to him by the incessant attacks of godless thieves from Cumberland.

On the other hand, the English raider not only professed to be actuated by principles of the highest honour, but, affecting an altogether superior civilisation, he looked down upon the Scots as unworthy of a place in the ranks of humanity, mere cut-throats and vermin to be ruthlessly exterminated.

It was notable that from whichever side of the Border the raider came he was never an aggressor, but always an unfortunate victim in search of his lost live stock. Even when the long catalogue of his own delinquencies in the shape of burnings, reivings, and slaughterings was proved beyond all doubt, he was never at a loss for a plea of justification, protesting that the head and front of his offending was merely the just recovery of that which had been forcibly stolen, if he had accidentally carried away a few head of nolt here and there which had never been his, the mistake could easily be explained, inasmuch as the difficulty of identification in the hot centre of the inevitable fight for his property obliged him to lift the lot, when able to do so, in order that their identity might be honestly and carefully considered when he had got them home. As to the other trifling complaints against him for the few fatal swings of his axe which had landed on the pates of his adversaries in the settlement of the business, they might be well excused, if not extolled, on the ground that he had rid the country of so many criminals. As a matter of fact, the raider's innocent endeavour to recover his lost cattle invariably took the form of a clean sweep of the largest herd of live stock he could lift, without the slightest consideration as to ownership.

CHAPTER X

BUCCLEUCH AND KINMONT WILLIE

THERE was no exploit on the Border more stirring and romantic than the rescue of 'Kinmont Willie' from Carlisle Castle near the end of the sixteenth century, a dramatic account of which we have in the well-known lengthy ballad. Kinmont was a descendant of the laird of Gilnockie, and seems to have inherited a considerable share of his forcible qualities for he is described as one of the most remarkable men who had emerged from the turmoil of Border warfare. He had a large and well-armed following, and conducted his raids with a skill which spread dismay among his enemies. As a leader he was absolutely fearless, ever in the front of the foray, dealing deadly strokes of his axe among the heads of his enemies. For his warden he cared no more than for the meanest of his retainers, having at all times strength enough to set him at defiance. The warden, however, was little disposed to exert his lawful authority over Kinmont, whom he admired and secretly encouraged in his depredations on the English side of the Border. This support from the warden became in time so notorious that Lord Hunsdon boldly accused King James himself of secretly encouraging this irresistible freebooter. He writes thus: 'Four hundred horsemen came and destroyed the town of Hawden Brig, whereat King James pretended to be very angry, and yet since that raid Will of Kinmont, who was the principal leader in it, hath been with the King in his cabinet above an hour, and on his departure the King gave him 100 crowns, little as he hath. What justice are we to look for at the King's hands let her Majesty judge'[1]. It is not surprising that Kinmont, feeling that he had both King and warden at his back, should have continued his invasions of Cumberland with unabated enthusiasm. These raids became so serious that Lord Scrope, the English warden, resolved to crush Kinmont at whatever cost, hence the remarkable incident which has rescued Kinmont's name from oblivion. If Kinmont had been fairly captured and hanged no fault could have been found with the English warden, but it was the meanness and treachery of his arrest which could not be tolerated. Kinmont had been present at Day Home, near Kershope Foot, on the occasion of a day of truce in the month of March, 1596 On the completion of the business which had called the Borderers together, Kinmont and his friends were returning to their homes as they believed in perfect security, every man throughout the wardenry being immune from arrest according to the time-honoured custom which had now hardened up into a well-observed march law.

In making their way down the right bank of the river Liddel, Kinmont and his followers were suddenly surprised by a troop of 200 light horse, under the command of Salkeld, the deputy English warden. Kinmont fled, but was overtaken and seized, and, by order of Salkeld, tied to the body of his own horse and carried in triumph to Carlisle Castle.

> They band his legs beneath his steed,
> They tied his hands behind his back,
> They guarded him five on each side,
> And they brought him ower the Liddel rack.
>
> They led him through the Liddel rack,
> And also through the Carlyle sands;
> They brought him to Carlyle Castle,
> To be at my lord Scrope's command.

[1] *Border Papers*, vol. i., p. 282.

This gross violation of the most sacred of the Border laws raised a howl of execration on all hands, for if the guarantee of freedom from arrest during the day of truce was no longer trustworthy the Warden's Court might cease to exist.

Besides, the deed was greatly aggravated by the weak excuse Scrope unwisely made in justification of his conduct. As the case had roused the Bold Buccleuch to anger, and was likely to lead to serious complications, the English warden put forth this lame explanation: 'How Kinmont was taken', he says, 'will appear by the attestations of his takers, which, if true, it is held that Kinmont did thereby break the assurance that day taken, and for his offences ought to be delivered to the officer against whom he offended, to be punished according to his discretion. Another reason for detaining him is his notorious enmity to this office, and the many outrages lately done by his followers. He appertains not to Buccleuch, but dwells out of his office, and was also taken beyond the limits of his charge, so Buccleuch makes the matter a mere pretext to defer justice and do further indignities'[1].

The assertion that Kinmont had broken the assurance taken before the Warden's Court was unsupported by a single grain of proof. Indeed, his one unpardonable offence was his notorious hostility to Lord Scrope and his officials.

As to the general charge of outrages committed by Kinmont and his followers, it must not be forgotten that all those assembled at the Warden's Court on the the day of truce, including the wardens themselves, were more or less tarred with the same stick, and might all have been arrested on the same general charge. The only difference between Kinmont and others lay in his superlative courage and success in a game in which they were all actively engaged. The very fact that Scrope was obliged to take him by an

[1] *Border Papers*, vii., p. 115.

act of treachery, though his stronghold was only a few miles distant from Carlisle Castle, is significant proof of Kinmont's power.

Notwithstanding the angry threats and blusters of Lord Scrope, Buccleuch insisted upon redress for the violation of the Border truce. He appealed to King James, and an application was made to the English government, who began the usual practice of evasion and delay. All the while Scrope was making preparations to end the dispute by hanging his prisoner on Haribee Hill.

As there was no time to be lost, and peaceful negotiations being useless, Buccleuch determined to secure Kinmont by force, and with this intent he called together a band of the bravest and most reliable of his followers and allies, numbering over two hundred men. They assembled at the Tower of Morton, about nine miles north-west of Carlisle, and among them were Walter Scott of Goldielands, Walter Scott of Harden, John Elliot of Copeshaw, the lairds of Whitehaugh and Mangerton, four sons of Kinmont, John of the Hollows, Christie of Barngleese, Roby of Langholm, and last, not least, a stalwart warrior from the English side of the Border, Hutchin Graham of Gards[1].

The expedition left Morton Tower on a dark and stormy night, thunder and lightning were incessant as they rode along and crossed the flooded waters of the Esk and Eden. Probably the tempestuous weather had slackened the vigilance of the nightwatch, for when the besiegers approached the castle walls they found it easy to take the first important step without discovery. Finding the postern, they rapidly undermined it, until the breach was wide enough to admit of men crawling through. Buccleuch was among the first inside, and in a moment the drowsy watch were overpowered and bound. The postern was wrenched open from the inside, admitting

[1] *Border Papers.*

a large party of the besiegers, who rushed to the castle prison, while Buccleuch held the postern. The door of Kinmont's cell was smashed, and Willie, heavily ironed, was brought forth, and borne along in triumph! the besiegers breaking the silence of the night by the blare of trumpets and shouts of defiance. The alarm spread throughout the town, where soon all was in confuson and dismay. Alarm bells were rung, the beacon lights blazed up, and answering beacons leapt into light on all the surrounding towers and hills. The garrison and people were so completely taken by surprise, and terror-struck with the warlike tumult, blended with the roll of thunder, that they shrank out of sight, thinking the day of judgment was upon them. Scrope wisely kept within his chamber, but Willie, borne upon the shoulders of Red Rowan, shouted a roaring good-night to him while passing under his window.

Without the loss of a single man, the party rode direct to Kinmont, calling at a blacksmith's shop on the way, where Willie was relieved of his load of iron fetters.

The indignation of Scrope almost unmanned him. No such disgrace had ever befallen the keeper of a strong English fortress. Buccleuch was denounced with all his accomplices, and Elizabeth was appealed to to compel King James to arrest and hand him over, 'that he might be punished as her Majesty might find that the quality of his offence merited'. It was, however, more the indignity to himself than the affront to Elizabeth which lay at the bottom of Scrope's desire for vengeance. Buccleuch defended his conduct with unanswerable clearness of argument and a plain statement of facts. He explained that he had exhausted all other means for securing justice, and in his peaceful endeavours he had met with little courtesy. The moment approached when the prisoner must either be rescued by force or perish unjustly upon the scaffold; but he and his Borderers had

CARLISLE CASTLE

refrained from all attack upon life or property, though he might have captured Scrope and all his garrison.

Elizabeth, indifferent to the Borderer's sense of fidelity regarding the question of truce, imperiously demanded the surrender of Buccleuch; but James took a leaf out of Elizabeth's own book in adopting the methods of evasion and delay. He was too much in Elizabeth's power to send a definite refusal, but the whole of his subjects, including the ministers of the kirk, were sternly opposed to the giving up to certain death of their chief of greatest fame.

A correspondence of interest took place, in which Elizabeth showed the same relentless thirst for the blood of Buccleuch which had so stained her womanhood in the case of Northumberland.

In one of her letters to James she seems to have had some difficulty in giving full expression to her bitter feelings within the limits of moderation.

The rescue of this noted prisoner from the great Northern fortress by a handful of moss-troopers was an insult to the Crown which could not be endured, and although James had endeavoured to appease her wrath by confining Buccleuch in Blackness Castle, she still continued to expostulate and insist upon his surrender to her. 'I beseech you', she says, 'to consider the greatness of my dishonour, and measure his just delivery accordingly. Deal in this case like a king that will have all this realm and others adjoining. See how justly and kindly you both can and will use a prince of my quality.

'For Border matters they are shameful and inhuman as it would loathe a king's heart to think of them.

'I have borne for your quiet too long, even murders committed by the hands of your own Wardens, which, if they be true, as I fear they be, I hope they shall well pay for such demerits, and you will never endure such barbarous acts to be unrevenged.'

Negotiations were carried on between the two

governments for many months, but James, greatly as he dreaded Elizabeth, was too fond of Buccleuch to comply with her demand. Meanwhile Scrope, burning for revenge on those who had, by their cunning and daring, turned him and his garrison into objects of ridicule, gathered together a force of two thousand men and invaded Liddesdale, laying the countryside in ashes, and committing horrible barbarities among those who were least implicated in the famous rescue. We are told by the Scottish Commissioners that 'they burned 24 onsettis of houses and carried off all the goods within four miles of bounds. They coupled the men, their prisoners, twa and twa, tageather in leashe like doggis. Of barnes and women, three or four score, they stripped off their clothis and sarkis leaving them naked in that sort, exposed to the injury of wind and weather, whereby nine or ten infants perished within eight days thereafter.'

In answer to this indictment the English Commissioners attempted to cover Lord Scrope's ravages by what they thought a sufficient plea of justification. 'It is no novelty', they say, 'but an ancient custom, for the warden to assist his opposite, and the Keeper of Liddesdale to ride on and "harrie" such theavis and on occasion to do so at his own hand.

'Buccleuch, besides surprising the second fortress of the Queen's Border, slaying twenty of her subjects, including sixteen of her soldiers, has bound himself with all the notorious raiders in Liddesdale, Eskdale and Ewesdale, and after asserting that he paid "out of his own purse" half of the sworn bill of Tynedale of £800 which the King commanded him to answer, joined himself with the Elliots and Armstrongs to plunder Tynedale for demanding the balance, slaying in their own houses seven of the Charletons and Dodds the chief claimants. And being imprisoned by the King, he made a sporting time of it, hunting and hawking, and on his realease did worse than ever, maintaining his cousins, Will of Hard Skarth, Watt of Harden, &c., to murder, burn and spoil as before. The people under his charge, Elliots, Armstrongs, Nicksons, &c., have of late years murdered above 50 of the Queen's good subjects, many in their own houses, on their lawful business at daytime—and 6 honest Allandale men going to Hexham Market were cut to pieces.

'For each of the last ten years, they have spoiled the West and Middle Marches of £5000. In short they are intolerable, and redress being unattainable, though repeatedly demanded by the Queen and warden, the justifiable reprisal ordered by her Majesty in necessary defence of her Border cannot in equity be called invasion, but rather honourable and neighbour-like assistance to maintain the inviolable amitie between the Princes and realms, against the proud violators thereof in either nation. To conclude, this action of the Lord Scrope is to be reputed and judged a "pune" [an ancient Border term] intending no other than a reprisal, which albeit of late years her Majesty's peaceable justice hath restrained.' In these fine plausible phrases about 'honourable and neighbour-like assistance' the Commissioners made what they probably thought a reasonable and conclusive answer to a charge of the most revolting barbarities inflicted upon helpless women and children who were left naked among the ruins of their homes, while others were led in leashes like dogs.

CHAPTER XI

EMBARRASSMENT OF KING JAMES

BUCCLEUCH'S confinement in Blackness Castle was of short duration, and no sooner had he regained his freedom than he began to devote the whole of his energies towards avenging the cruelties inflicted by Scrope upon the women and children of Liddesdale.

Along with his ally, Ker of Cessford, one of the most renowned freebooters of his day, he marched into Northumberland with fifty horse and one hundred foot. He burned and destroyed three hundred onsteads and dwellings and recovered a large number of the cattle recently taken from Liddesdale.

To this invasion there seems to have been little or no opposition, for the Warden of the East Marches had received no support from the government since the days of Lord Northumberland, and now he found himself so helpless that he appealed to Burleigh in language of unmistakable force regarding the miserable plight to which the Border defence had been reduced. In his letter he declared that he could not find six able horses within the wardenry to follow the fray, and when he had been assured of the help of 300 foot not 100 were forthcoming, and these were literally naked. 'Wishing to God', he says, 'I had never lived to serve where neither her Majesty nor her officer is obeyed.'

What made this raid peculiarly heinous in the eyes of Elizabeth, was the fact that Commissioners were at that moment engaged in negotiating a treaty in regard to Border troubles, now rendered acute by the successful assault upon Carlisle Castle. As a matter of course the Queen demanded the immediate surrender into her hands of both Buccleuch and Cessford. Buccleuch defended his conduct, declaring that the inroad into Tynedale was amply justified, as the Liddesdale men had just been raided by 60 Tynedale men, who had carried off an immense herd of cattle and sheep.

He and the neighbouring gentlemen had only followed the usual custom of 'hot trod', tracking the thieves with hound and horn until they were finally discovered at the place where the booty was housed. The thieves were offered both life and goods if the cattle were restored, which they having obstinately refused, their doors were burned down and the booty recovered. This explanation was not enough for Elizabeth, who declared that the time had gone past for 'excuses, differings, and lingerings.' That Buccleuch, who was described as 'God's curse,' had gone ravaging with fire and sword into Northumberland while his former evil deeds were as yet unpunished, and James was threatened with direful consequences to both himself and Scotland if her demands were not complied with. This storm, however, James believed would blow over, if he could only negotiate, and delay until the force of the tempest had spent itself. Buccleuch was one of his greatest favourites, and both King and Council secretly approved of all his late exploits on the Border. Indeed, no sooner had he finished his last invasion than he rode to Edinburgh, where he had an interview with his Sovereign, when the two of them 'laughed long and loud on the purpose.'

The Council drew up a defence excusing the Tynedale invasion, on the ground that it was a legitimate reprisal for an English raid into Scotland a short time before, and the slaughter complained of was confined to malefactors, enemies to the public weal and quiet of both countries.

This time, however, it was clear that Elizabeth was inexorable, and as she plainly intimated her determination to declare war if the procrastination continued, the King found himself in a situation of considerable perplexity. A war between the two kingdoms he knew would be fatal to Scotland, as she had neither men nor money to oppose the great military strength of Elizabeth, while to himself it might be disastrous, inasmuch as it might imperil his claim to the succession.

Buccleuch, thoroughly understanding the King's dilemma, loyally determined to run all risks and place himself at Elizabeth's disposal, to which King James was reluctantly compelled to consent.

He therefore gave himself up to Sir William Bowes, who conducted him to Berwick, where he was handed over to the keeping of Sir John Cary, the governor of the town. Sir John undertook the charge of the dauntless Borderer with a reluctance almost amounting to terror, if we may judge from the anxious letter he addressed to Lord Hunsdon upon the subject. 'I entreat your lordship', he says, 'that I may not become the jailor of so dangerous a prisoner, or at least that I may know whether I may keep him a prisoner or no, for there is not a worse or more dangerous place in England to keep him in than this; it is so near his friends, and besides so many in this town willing to pleasure him, and his escape may be so easily made, and once out of the town he is past recovery. Wherefore I humbly beseech your honour let him be removed from hence to a more secure place, for I protest to the Almighty God, before I will take the charge to keep him here, I will desire to be put in prison myself, and to have a keeper of me. For what care soever be had of him here, he shall want no furtherance whatsoever wit of man can devise, if he himself list to make an escape. So I pray your lordship, even for God's sake and the love of a brother, to relieve me from this danger'[1].

[1] *Border Papers*, vii., 420.

Cary's terror of his uncanny prisoner was soon set at rest by the good sense and orderly conduct of Buccleuch, whose submission to captivity required no bolts or bars, being indeed a chivalrous sacrifice of his freedom in order that he might free his sovereign from what seemed an impending disaster.

Hearing what Buccleuch had done Sir Robert Ker showed his devotion by a similar surrender, but whether Elizabeth was impressed by the loyalty and courage of the prisoners, or some other unknown reason, she ceased to clamour for their punishment.

Soon they were both allowed to deliver their pledges and depart in peace.

After his liberation from prison Buccleuch became a completely changed man, resolved to abandon the evils of raiding, and, as Keeper of Liddesdale, to check the mosstroopers by all the means within his power. He was the first great Border chief who, in those rude times, began to entertain statesmanlike views of his country's permanent interests and destiny, and whatever may have been the deficiencies of his methods in curbing the excesses among the Armstrongs and the Elliots—excesses which he himself had so recently encouraged—yet there can be little doubt that his rule during the last years of Elizabeth's reign exercised a great and valuable influence in the direction of law and order. Being convinced that nothing less than a radical reformation of the evil customs prevalent on the Border must be made before the slightest hope could be entertained of improvement in the social and economic conditions of the people, he determined to use his whole official power in laying the foundation of orderly government and honest dealing.

This was no easy task for one so notoriously famed as himself in the great game he now sought to condemn. All his old allies turned against him with the utmost bitterness, and would gladly have accomplished his overthrow if they had dared to grapple with his resolute valour and his iron will.

Steadily he progressed with his reforms, and did more good in the way of social regeneration on the Scottish Border than any man of that day.

Soon he was received at the Court of Elizabeth with considerable favour, as she had already heard 'golden opinions' of his splendid efforts to pacify the wild Borders.

It was a memorable occasion when he, the breaker of Carlisle Castle, for whose blood Elizabeth had at one time thirsted, now stood before her. It is said that the Queen demanded of him, with a glance of those flaming eyes before which all men trembled, how he dared to storm her castle, to which Buccleuch replied, 'What, madam, is there that a brave man may not dare?' 'Ah!' said Elizabeth, pleased with the reply, and turning to her courtiers: 'Give me a thousand such leaders and I'll shake any throne in Europe.'

CHAPTER XII

ACCESSION OF KING JAMES

During the last half of the sixteenth century the clan of Graham increased greatly in number, occupying nearly the whole of Eskdale from Gilnockie to the Solway. There was among them, at the death of Elizabeth in 1603, a certain proportion of reivers of the incorrigible type, but also a great many who had gladly settled down to tillage as a happier means of existence than the endless broil and hardships of the foray.

From the earliest records of the Border Grahams we have evidence of their settlement in Canonbie early in the thirteenth century. Sir John Graham, who had inherited the whole of Upper Eskdale from his great-grandfather, Sir Roger Avenal (who died in 1243), granted to the monks of Canonbie, for the repose of the soul of his wife, all the lands of Hollows, Brockwoodlees, Rowanburn, Limycleuch, Nettyholm, Torquoon, Batenbank, Einthorn, Bilmans Knowe, etc [1].

These lands were held by the Cell of Canonbie for the most part until the year 1539. On October the 18th in that year George and John Graham were summoned to appear before Queen Mary and her Council to settle a dispute between them as to which was entitled to the fruits and profits of Canonbie [2], so that nine years after Gilnockie's death we find the

---
[1] *Chronica de Mailros*, p. 155.
[2] Priory of Canonbie, Armstrong's *Liddesdale*, p. 115.

Graham's contending for their territorial rights within the debateable land.

In 1552 the clan numbered 500 warriors, sturdy defenders of the Border, inhabiting thirteen strong towers, eight of which lay between Esk and Leven. The leader to whom their ancient fame as a fighting clan was largely due was William Graham of Stuble, known as 'Lang Will', a man of immense size and muscular strength, combined with a commanding personality. He seems to have been one of those masterful spirits, like Gilnockie, thrown upon the surface in lawless times to control and direct the actions of the most untameable of men—an instrument capable of infinite mischief, but equally capable of great good if wisely enlisted on the side of law and order.

On the whole, we may infer that the ascendency of Lang Will was patriotic and pleasing to his sovereign, for we find that his son Fergus of Mote (according to Stothard's *Book of Scottish Heraldry*) had arms granted to him in 1555.

William Graham, son of Fergus, and grandson of Lang Will, born in 1563, was dispossessed of his paternal acres by King James in 1605, banished without trial or warning, but returned to Eskdale, and died at Dykehead in 1657 after a life of merciless persecution.

There is some uncertainty as to the date of the clan's settlement in Cumberland, but it seems probable that they were forced southward by the gradual ascendency of the Armstrongs, with whom they were long at feud within the debateable land. Their most ancient strongholds in Cumberland were Mote and Netherby. The former stood upon a lofty and, on one side, an almost inaccessible ridge of red rock, the site of an ancient Roman camp, overhanging the river Liddle near its confluence with the Esk. On the north side of the river was the debateable land in which Graham of Mote claimed the right of tillage, which led to frequent disputes before the wardens. Nearly all trace of their once formidable strength has now disappeared.

A little further south, at some distance from the river, stands the stately modern mansion of Netherby, built upon, or near, the site of the ancient tower, and still the home of the Grahams. It stands amid charming surroundings of hanging woods and peaceful grass lands, in wondrous contrast to the brawl and revelry, the hot pursuit of hue and cry which awoke the echoes of the vale three hundred years ago.

These were the strongholds of the two most noted chiefs of the Eskdale Grahams when, by the death of Queen Elizabeth, the kingdoms were united and the conditions so changed that reiving and raiding could no longer be endured.

But before proceeding to relate the extraordinary barbarity with which the last of the great clans was suppressed, it becomes necessary to draw the reader's attention to the evil conditions in politics, religion, and morality, and to the unworthy men at the head of affairs in England, in order to show how such impolitic and savage cruelties became possible.

Notwithstanding the long period of suspense and the many conjectures regarding the succession which had disturbed men's minds during the last years of Elizabeth's life, when the critical hour at last arrived the Crown of England passed from the great house of Tudor to that of Stuart as peacefully as it ever did from father to son. The whole nation seemed overjoyed and clamorous to give James a cordial reception. As he passed from town to town in his royal progress to London all classes flocked about him, allured by interest or curiosity.

Great were the acclamations on all sides, for somehow or other the people had got an impression that he was the wisest man of his age, that his throne would be established in righteousness, with the good and faithful of the land for ever around it, and that justice and mercy would literally cling to his sceptre. The King at last had come who would soften or repeal all the harsh statutes enforced by the Government of Elizabeth.

About this time throughout Western Europe, but notably in England, there was a rising sense of uneasiness and discontent in men's minds regarding the unlimited use of the royal prerogative, which in the hands of Elizabeth had been stretched into even the most private concerns of her subjects. But the great success of her rule, both at home and abroad, rendered her sovereignty popular in spite of the iron severity with which she restrained the rising spirit of freedom. King James, however, had neither the understanding to perceive, nor the capacity to check, the advance of enlarged and comprehensive ideas of human freedom. His inordinate vanity was so inflated by the warmth of his reception in England, that he forthwith began to establish within his own mind a speculative system of absolute government, which he firmly believed, to use his own words, none of his subjects 'save traitors and rebels would make any scruple to admit'. His learning was allowed to be considerable, but of political courage, or even the rudimentary conceptions of statesmanship, he was destitute; feeble in temper, wrong and obstinate in his judgments, and frequently exposed to ridicule from the preposterous exhibitions of his vanity, his subjects soon began to realise that their new monarch was 'the most learned fool in all creation'. His character has been delineated by some of the historians in language which almost savours of pure abuse. Lingard tells us that it was melancholy and mischievous that monarchy should be so degraded by the existence of this unworthy creature upon the throne of England in succession to the great Elizabeth. He was silly in his conversation and bearing, jealous of his authority, confused and per-

plexed about trifles, and without sufficient dignity to
restrain him from conduct akin to clowning. From
Balfour we have some humorous details of his
personal appearance and ordinary habits: 'He was
of middle stature', he tells us, 'more corpulent by
reason of his clothes than his body. These clothes
were large and easy, the doublets so quilted as to be
stiletto proof, and his breeches were made in large
pleats, fully stuffed. He was naturally of a timorous
disposition, which was the great reason for his padded
doublets. His eyes were large and staring, and so
rolled and ogled at strangers who came into his
presence that they were glad to leave the room,
being stared out of countenance. His beard was
thin and his tongue too large for his mouth, so that
his drinking was uncomely, the liquid escaping on
each side of his cup. He never washed his hands,
but only rubbed his finger-ends slightly with the
wet end of a napkin. His legs were weak, having
had some foul play in his youth, or rather before he
was born, so that he was unable to stand at seven
years of age. That weakness caused him to be ever
leaning on the shoulders of other men.'

In spite of all historical criticisms however, which
in his case are somewhat conflicting, it seems probable
that James was not destitute of good intentions, but
was simply so intoxicated with the consciousness of
his greatness that he lost all sense of proportion in
thinking of himself and the rest of humanity. In
Scotland he had lived almost in poverty—a pensioner
of Queen Elizabeth—but when seated on the throne
of Great Britain he fancied himself in possession of
power and wealth which no extravagance could
exhaust. He could never be got to understand that
the great authority enjoyed by Elizabeth was the
outcome of her own remarkable powers of brain and
profound knowledge of statecraft, and not to be
ascribed, as he thought, entirely to regal birth and
title. Nor did he ever cease to cherish the conviction

that all regal power within the realm centred in his own person by hereditary and divine right. In comparing himself with other European sovereigns, he argued that as he bore the same rank he was entitled to the same prerogatives as though England had passed through all the conflicts and innovations, supported by military power, which had established absolute despotism in other countries.

Intoxicated as he was with these sublime conceptions of his omnipotence, he ventured to entertain Parliament on one famous occasion with his views regarding his kingly office. 'Kings', he said, 'were, in his opinion, the representatives and images of God. Like Him they could make and unmake, exalt and debase, give life or death. Like Him they were judges of all, but accountable to none; and like Him they claimed both the affection of the souls and the services of the bodies of their subjects. If it were blasphemy to deny the power of God, so it was sedition to deny the power of the king.' On another occasion he finished an address to the Commons as follows: 'I conclude the point touching the power of kings with this axiom of divinity, "To dispute what God may do is blasphemy, but what God wills *that* divines may lawfully, and do ordinarily, dispute and discuss, so it is sedition in subjects to dispute what the king may do in the height of his power."' Yet while holding on to these preposterous claims, he innocently thought it unnecessary to make the smallest provision, either in force or politics, to support them. In point of fact, he imagined that his intellectual endowments were so transcendant that he could achieve the absolute rule to which he aspired by the mere force of argument and eloquence. So entirely satisfied was he of his mental supremacy, that he boldly proclaimed himself the most learned scholar and the most profound philosopher of the age in which he lived—that is, the age of Bacon, Shakespeare, Ben Jonson, Spenser,

Raleigh, Leicester, Drake, and a host of others whose genius still lights up the world with imperishable lustre.

One can well imagine how it must have tickled the sense of humour of some of those intellectual giants on hearing James' authoritative declaration that he was the only safe guide in all the spiritual as well as the material interests of his subjects, his long and wearisome directions to preachers, his confutation of the heresies of foreign divines, his demonstration of the existence of witches, and his sermons on the mischiefs of demonology.

It was the age of witchcraft in Great Britain, and it remained for this paragon of wisdom to contribute by his writings and his supreme authority to the hardening up of this ignorant terror into an article of religious belief, at a time when knowledge was beginning to dispel the mists of superstition.

In his treatise on the subject he declared that such detestable crimes as evil enchantment should be punished with death, regardless of age, sex, or rank, according to the law of God, the civil, the imperial, and municipal laws of all Christian nations. The barbarous laws he had established in Scotland became the laws of England also, soon after the Union, and many hundreds of unfortunate creatures in both countries suffered an ignominious death for an impossible offence. Though neither age, sex, or rank was spared, it was usually the most helpless and inoffensive, such as aged and lone women, who were most exposed to its deadly operation. Men called 'witch hunters' were regularly employed to ferret out and bring to punishment those who, from living a retired life, were suspected of witchcraft, and who were liable to be denounced and burned for any accident or misfortune occurring in their locality.

One witch-finder called Mathew Hopkins, residing at Manningtree, in Essex, was extolled for his great zeal and success in hunting out and bringing to the stake no fewer than sixty reputed witches within his own county in one year, all old, ignorant, helpless women, who could neither plead their own cause nor hire an advocate to plead for them.

The most damning proof of guilt was said to have been invented by King James himself, and always strongly recommended by him. It was the tying together of the thumbs and the toes of a suspected person and pitching her into the river. If she floated she was pronounced guilty, and at once taken out and burned to death; but if she sank it was accepted as proof of her innocence, and in that case she was *only drowned*. The reason which James assigned for this original method of arriving at the truth was, to use his own words, 'As some persons had renounced their baptism by water, so water refuses to receive them.'

From the commencement of his reign James had surrounded himself with a motley crowd of almost ragged Scotch nobility (his friends of humbler times), upon whom he lavished wealth and honours, and entertained with a costly splendour far beyond all precedent. This he continued, apparently unconscious of the damage to his popularity, and the serious spread of resentment among all classes of his subjects. To forget his cares in the hurry of the chase, or in carousing at table, or laughing at the buffoonery of boon companions seem to have constituted the chief pleasures of his life. One may readily imagine how the immortal creator of Falstaff and Malvolio must have roared over the extraordinary pantomime going on with all regal equipments, and how he must have longed to utilise both King Jamie and Gingling Geordy for the boards of the Globe Theatre, even at the risk of arrest for *lèse majesté*.

My object in drawing special attention to this unprecedented compound of humanity, who held supreme power throughout those woeful years 1605 and 1606, is to explain how it came about that such strange and fantastic barbarities were possible at that special juncture in our history. To be just to James, however, it is only fair to state that he sincerely desired that the union should be genuine—that the two kingdoms should lay aside their ancient hostility and accept a perfect incorporation, which would make all his subjects amenable to the same laws, and above all, thankful to God for having sent them at last a ruler, the incarnation of wisdom, before whom every subject in both countries could reverently bow his head. Far from making allowance he had not the faintest perception of the prejudices, the entangled web of mutual hatreds and feuds, which time alone could modify or extinguish. Of the trend of public opinion he knew nothing, made light of animosities which had been growing for ages, obstinately believing that the laws and institutions of a people could be changed at once by royal decree.

He was not long in finding that his plan of complete union was disdainfully rejected by the Scotch, to whom the idea was strongly suggestive of national subjection, and by the English, who saw in it an invitation to a still greater influx of those needy northern sponges, whom the King's extravagant liberality had already crowded into London, to the disgust and resentment of all classes.

Above all, the English nobility were indignant at the pretensions of the poverty-stricken peers of Scotland to precedence, according to the antiquity of their titles, which James had readily conceded.

The proposals of James were therefore received with silent opposition by the English parliament, and with frankly-expressed aversion by the Scotch. He addressed the House of Commons by letter, and he harangued them in person, but all his eloquence fell upon deaf ears, merely provoking angry discussions, in which his own conduct escaped not criticism, while the foulest aspersions were thrown upon the national character of his countrymen. The pride of those

Scotchmen now residing in England was kindled into a blaze, for while they were feeding upon the bounty of England, they loftily pretended to scorn the benefits which were begrudged them by the meanness of Englishmen, who failed to appreciate the advantages of their distinguished presence round the throne.

The more ardent King James appeared in promoting his scheme of union, the more reluctant was the English parliament to consider it, and the more convinced became the public that his zeal was prompted by his notorious partiality for his own countrymen.

James was deeply mortified at the failure of all his efforts towards complete incorporation, and enraged that every step he had taken towards the enlargement and consolidation of the royal prerogative had been met by a stubborn determination to curtail, rather than to extend, its limits.

He was also beset with the wild storm of religious fanaticism which was raging throughout the land, and over all Western Europe, for it was a time when the slightest provocation was sufficient to embroil the leading nations in war.

In addition to religious contests, there were deadly evils arising from the degraded moral and social condition of an enormous proportion of the people of every class.

We are told that notwithstanding the greatly increased power and prestige of England under Elizabeth, there had been no improvement in the manners and customs of her subjects.

About the time of her death the conditions of life in many parts of the country had become absolutely intolerable, crime stalked rampant throughout the land, and the law was powerless to grapple with it. While the lower orders in the larger towns killed and robbed with brutal violence, the upper classes (including members of the highest nobility), stabbed and murdered each other on the most frivolous pretences.

It was the custom for every gentleman to swagger about well armed, and when staggering from tavern to tavern his sword leaped from its scabbard on the slightest provocation. But in addition to brawling and bloodshed the worst forms of fraud and rascality were practised among men of family with high-sounding names. Deliberate and systematic robberies, involving even secret assassinations, were planned and carried out, in order to procure funds for indulgence in idleness and debauchery. At no period of English history was the respectable citizen in a more miserable minority! Honours and rewards went forth to knaves and worthless favourites, while the honest and industrious were held in contempt and taxed and robbed of their means. So lavish was King James in the bestowal of knighthood that the distinction ceased to be a mark of honour. Any nobleman in favour at Court could obtain the title for his agents or retainers almost as a kind of perquisite to which his station entitled him.

Occasionally, indeed, an impecunious lordling has been known to procure the dignity in order to stave off a pressing creditor. And so reckless was James in scattering it about that on one occasion, shortly after his accession to the English throne, he knighted seven hundred in one week. In consequence of this cheapening of the title, many of those who had fairly earned distinction by meritorious public service, declined to accept the dignity, which so affronted the King that, with his blunt perception of absurdity, he promptly imposed a fine of five hundred pounds upon his deserving subject. Finally the title became so draggled in the mud that in nearly every jail delivery a 'Sir Thomas', a 'Sir James', or a 'Sir William' was found among the delinquents, and the public had the edifying spectacle of seeing gentlemen whom their sovereign had delighted to honour, dangling at the rope's end in expiation of abominable crimes. Another title came into existence in this reign, said to have been invented by Lord Salisbury at a moment when James' monstrous extravagance had reduced the finances to their lowest ebb. This was the baronetcy, which was intended to be an inferior grade of nobility — a kind of hereditary knighthood to be strictly confined to 200, for which a thousand pounds each was demanded. It was a device by which Salisbury reckoned upon a return of £200,000 to the impoverished exchequer. It was to be purely a case of purchase—first come, first served, after the manner of allotment of shares in a limited company. The applications for the honour were most disappointing. At first only a small number were taken up, though in later years the market improved, and the demand became so brisk that the original limit was set aside.

CHAPTER XIII

THE KING'S PASSION FOR FAVOURITES

SUCH were the evil conditions existing in England when the complicated Border question, fraught with so many dangerous possibilities, came up demanding solution.

The union of the two kingdoms under one sovereign, as a matter of course involved the abolition of the frontier with all its machinery of Warden's Courts and the laws and customs of centuries, but, above all, the suppression or reformation of the raider or mosstrooper.

What had hitherto been the marches between the two kingdoms were henceforth to be known as the Middle Marches in the heart of the newly united country, with Carlisle as the chief centre of honest trading. There it was intended that Armstrongs and Elliots were to meet Grahams, Musgraves, and Forsters in friendly intercourse for the settlement of all future cattle transactions in good coin of the realm. All slayings, thievings, fire-raisings, and deadly feuds were to pass away like an evil dream, and all the methods of a highly advanced civilisation were to spring into activity on a certain date, and at a certain hour, by order of the royal Solomon.

It is, however, somewhat difficult to believe that King James really imagined the possibility of a settlement, by a mere stroke of his royal pen, of all the wrongs, and griefs, and hatreds, both private and public, which had disturbed that unsettled land for ages.

No one could have had a more intimate knowledge of Border complications from personal experience than himself, as we have seen in his dealings with the bold Buccleuch. Moreover, he had made several raids of a punitive character through Canonbie and Liddesdale, in all of which he had completely failed to secure the offenders, though he had spread ruin and desolation among the very class who deserved shelter and encouragement. The most notable of these foolish invasions to pacify the Border was his expedition of 1597. On that occasion he made a prolonged stay at Dumfries at the head of a large body of troops, and from this base he scoured the country round for many miles, falling upon the inhabitants with indiscriminate slaughter.

His time being limited, reasonable investigation of the rights and wrongs of individuals was dispensed with. Most of those who suffered were the farmers and labourers who remained at their homes and were easily captured. If no specific offence could be proved against them, yet guilt might be assumed from the fact that their homes were within the area of the marauders' activities, and their surnames were suggestive of evil deeds. But whether they were friends or victims of the mosstrooper, James, having no time to discover, thought they would be 'nae the waur o' hanging.' He argued that as it was upon the corn and cattle raised by their industry that the malefactor subsisted, it seemed clear to him that if this means of support were destroyed, the raider must eventually starve. Following out this profound policy, many men were seized, and promptly hanged in presence of their weeping wives and children, who were left destitute among the ashes of their dwellings, while their cattle, food, and all their belongings, were swept away in the remorseless raid. In this memorable invasion it is curious to note how precisely history repeated itself, for the policy of James was exactly that of the Earl of Angus in the reign of

James the Fifth. He also deemed it sound policy to destroy the food producers in the hope of starving the raiders whom he failed to capture.

In both cases the evil was aggravated, as the raider, finding his supplies at home cut off, did the most natural thing under the circumstances; he simply widened the field of his operations, and extended his invasions both north and south to districts hitherto beyond the limits of raiding enterprise. In none of these punitive invasions were the reivers either checked in their operations or sensibly reduced in number. While King James was busy crushing the defenceless inhabitants of Annandale and Eskdale, the real offenders easily retired to their safe hinterland, where the soldiers had no desire to follow them.

They not only retired scatheless to the hills, but had the boldness to return while James was still at work among the tillers of the soil, and surprised and humiliated him by repeated and successful attacks upon his followers in the vicinity of his camp. They waylaid and killed Sir John Carmichael, the Scottish warden of the Western Marches while attending to his official duties at Langholm, in ostentatious defiance of the immediate presence of the sovereign and his imposing military force. The net result, therefore, of the blundering and barbarous invasion of 1597 was famine and desolation over a large district, with a considerable increase to the forces of disorder, for James had given convincing proof that laborious industry had more to fear at his hands than killing and thieving.

It will readily be seen how vain was the hope that the many Border evils and complexities could ever be unravelled and reformed humanely, justly, and firmly by a king who could so little realise the nature of the problem, and whose diseased vanity honestly led him to believe that he alone understood the question in all its details.

King Jamie 'was sae gifted with gifts o' grace excelled by nane' that he persistently acted upon the assumption that the poor Borderers were simply possessed of the devil; a race of men afflicted with a double dose of original sin, who deliberately rejected the saintly path of righteousness and starvation spread out before them, preferring to eat and drink and live by the iniquitous methods of their fathers and grandfathers.

With all his wisdom the King failed to perceive that the lawless condition of the Border was the natural outcome of ages of confusion and armed contention, when the poor Borderer could never reckon with any approach to certainty when his life would be safe or his belongings secure even for a day.

I have said so much about the absence of common sense and the mental and physical infirmities of this unique example of sovereignty that I am somewhat reluctant to pursue the subject further; only, as there were other deficiences in his character to which we can trace the fatal hurricane which swept the Grahams of Eskdale to their doom, a little further study of the man becomes necessary. One peculiarity in James was especially marked, and that was his complete indifference to his pledged word. In spite of his religious professions, he broke his word with as much facility as he gave it, and without the least appearance of shame; he was always ready to swear or to forswear, just as best suited his convenience.

Then, again, his erratic attention to his duties was productive of great confusion, loss, and injustice. He was always finding expedients to avoid the tedium of public business in the intensity of his craving for personal ease and amusement. Cases involving life or death were often hurriedly decided without being understood, amid the laughter and buffoonery of the choice spirits around him.

If James failed, however, to secure the love and

respect of his subjects, he could truly boast that he tickled their sense of humour as no sovereign had done since the days of Nero. There could be no complaint on that score, for his whole reign from first to last was leavened by the whimsicalities which are familiar to us in our modern comic operas. In nearly all his performances on State and other occasions he was so intensely laughable and grotesque that, in the universal roar of merriment at an exhibition of clowning among the seats of the mighty, men failed to give their serious attention to the gruesome realities of death and confiscations all the while running along amid tears and broken hearts, sadly at variance with the fantastic and side-splitting vagaries of the royal philosopher.

But above and beyond all other of the King's failings, that which had the most baneful consequences upon his country was his passionate craze for favourites. Obscure and often disreputable adventurers succeeded each other in his regard throughout the whole period of his reign. These favourites were raised to positions of place and authority over the heads of the leading statesmen of the day, quite regardless of the affront and discouragement to men upon whom the welfare of the country mainly depended. One of the most notorious of these upstarts, upon whom James lavished his maudlin affections, was Robert Carr, a young Scotchman of two and twenty. His only recommendation appears to have consisted in his marvellously good looks and graceful bearing. Of education he was almost destitute, being ignorant of the very rudiments of his own language, a circumstance in no way discomfiting to James, who in his fondness for the youth, rather regarded his ignorance as an advantage, as it gave him the golden opportunity of personally conducting Carr's education, and moulding his character in accordance with his own infallible methods. The King had persuaded himself that this piece of raw material, by deriving all sense, experience, and knowledge direct from himself—the fountain-head of wisdom and learning—would, in time, be so sage as to leave no room for any rival or competitor, and would thus be able to grapple with the most profound problems of government as never statesman had done in any age.

His devotion to Carr in time quite eclipsed the affection he bore to his own children, planting the seeds of that contempt and aversion with which his eldest son, Prince Henry, regarded him to the end of his short life.

While his education was in progress the young man was encouraged by the honours of knighthood and the peerage. He was created Viscount Rochester, brought into the Privy Council and adorned with the Garter. Riches were heaped upon him at a time when Lord Salisbury was at his wits' end for funds to keep the machinery of the State in motion, and with these riches came the power of indulgence in all those pleasures becoming a nobleman of his exalted rank. He became involved at an early period of his career in immoral relations with the young Countess of Essex, whom he ultimately married under scandalous circumstances, which drew forth an indignant remonstrance from Sir Thomas Overbury, in revenge for which Carr and his spouse speedily had him murdered.

Then came the downfall. In spite of his having further raised him to the Earldom of Somerset, James was obliged to abandon him, and thus he passed away into obscurity with his ridiculous titles.

The King's heart was not broken, however, for prior to the loss of Carr his soul had become filled with adoration for the ever memorable George Villiers. This young man was blessed with a face so beautiful and a figure so elegant that even Carr was eclipsed; in addition to these advantages he was gifted with a vigorous and attractive personality, combined with a will of his own, which the world has good reason to remember.

With the fascinations of young Villiers James became completely hypnotised, gradually surrendering to the superior force of his strong will, clinging to him, and ever hanging upon his shoulder with the same maudlin fondness he had bestowed upon the discarded Robert Carr. He gave him the pet name of 'Steenie' in the royal privacy, to which he was at all times admitted, and where he was allowed a freedom and familiarity which in time ripened into something of the nature of supremacy and masterdom. He was, however, far too practical a man to stand loitering with his master in the dreamy speculations of witchcraft while so many golden possibilities were beginning to fire his restless ambition. Nor had he long to wait for the gratification of his lofty aspirations. His devoted sovereign soon raised him to the peerage as Viscount, Earl, Marquis, and Duke of Buckingham, and while men were yet wrapped in wonder at these rapid and exorbitant honours, there came the distinction of the Garter, the Master of the Horse, Chief Justice of the King's Bench, Lord Warden of the Cinque ports, Steward of Westminster, Constable of Windsor, and Lord High Admiral of England. For none of these great offices was he qualified by education and training, except perhaps the mastership of the horse, and from all of them he received revenue which in the aggregate was enormous. So absolute was his ascendency over King James that for years he was practically the ruler of England, assuming the airs and splendour of royalty, and directing the exercise of the royal prerogative pretty much in accordance with his own will. This usurpation of the functions of sovereignty ultimately became intolerable, not only to Englishmen, but to the representatives of foreign courts, who so resented the intervention of Villiers between them and the monarch to whom they were accredited, that the entire 'corps diplomatique' united in offering a remonstrance to the King, an affront unique in the history of diplomacy. Carendolet, the Secretary of the Spanish legation, was commissioned to interview the King in the name of all the ambassadors, but so carefully guarded was James, that speech with him could only be obtained by stratagem.

When Carendolet found himself face to face with James he entertained him for a few minutes with the plainest speaking he had probably ever heard. He frankly told him that he was a prisoner in his own palace, surrounded by spies and informers in the pay of Buckingham, and that none of his servants dared to execute his orders, or to give their advice without the previous approbation of the Duke, and that the kingdom was no longer governed by its sovereign, but by a man who sought to gratify his private revenge by embroiling the country in unjust and impolitic quarrels. Not even the degradation of this scornful language could rouse James to a sense of his dignity, or shake his confidence in the indispensable Steenie whose pernicious counsel and base intrigues continued to stain the honour of England not only throughout the lifetime of James but far into the reign of 'Baby Charles.' At last, having compromised the honour of Anne of Austria, Queen of Louis XIII of France, Buckingham was assassinated by one Felton, but whether at the instigation of his enemies at the Court of France or in revenge for some wrong in his own country has never been clearly ascertained.

CHAPTER XIV

LORD CUMBERLAND AND THE CUMBRIAN GENTRY IN 1605

ONE of the most notable of the favourites of King James, after he mounted the English throne, was the Earl of Cumberland. He was probably not a favourite of the highest order like Carr or Villiers—not one of those upon whose shoulder the King hung with maudlin infatuation—but one in whom he discovered transcendent merits unobserved by the world at large. There is no record of any public service having been rendered by this nobleman calling for the princely rewards which James felt it incumbent on him to bestow. What shape those rewards took, and how they affected the Grahams of Eskdale, is disclosed in the documents to be found at Muncaster Castle and in other papers recently brought to light.

As a personage of the highest rank in the north country at the time of the union, Lord Cumberland filled the office of English warden in addition to that of Lord Lieutenant of Cumberland. The warden on the Scottish side, at that time, was Lord Holme, a friend of Cumberland, and from the glimpses we have of the rule of these two officers it would seem that their government was simply an organised system of plunder, unchecked, unreprimanded, and unpunished. It was clear, then, that there was no service sufficiently meritorious in Cumberland's official career in the north calling for the grateful recognition of his King and country. During his rule in the Western Marches he astutely foresaw that the impending suppression of the Border clans, consequent upon the Union, would lead to considerable changes in regard to tenure of land. As landlords under the ancient system the clansmen's days were numbered. He saw there would probably be an overhauling of titles and extensive confiscations, followed by a scramble for the acres of the dispossessed clansmen, and in that scramble Cumberland resolved to have the lion's share, to which he doubtless considered his social and political importance entitled him.

The disestablishment of the clansmen was a question of considerable complexity, and in order to deal justly with the deserving, a long and patient investigation was indispensable. Alas, such enquiries were wearisome to King James when impatient to confer his favours. Throughout life he acted on the principle that it was so much easier to transport or to hang a man than to think about him.

The government resolved to appoint a commission, ostensibly to pacify the Border and to find, if possible, some solution of the great problem which confronted the Union. It is note-worthy, however, that, before the commissioners were even selected, Lord Cumberland was allowed to prejudice the minds of the Privy Councillors by a fierce denunciation of all the owners of the coveted acres in Eskdale. They were represented as incorrigible criminals and oppressors, and the very name of Graham was said to be a terror to all the country round. Eskdale was called a hot centre for thieves and murderers, men beyond all hope of reformation, whose banishment or extermination was loudly demanded by all law-abiding citizens. These denunciations were confirmed by his lordship's friend the Earl of Northumberland (known as the Wizard Earl), who was lord of the manor of Cockermouth, and as a Cumbrian landowner, had substantial hopes of agrarian plunder for himself should the longed-for wave of confiscation haply flow in his direction. In addition to the evidence of Lord Northumberland, confirmatory letters were received from his agent, Sir Wilfred Lawson, whose eager vituperation of the Eskdale Grahams bore that decided tinge of malice suggestive of ancient family rivalry which might have given pause to men of thoughtful minds. In these letters Lawson declared that it only required the removal of the hated clan of Graham to make the Borderland as peaceful as any other part of His Majesty's dominions; thereby implying that Armstrongs, Elliots, Musgraves, Taylors, and other reivers, were amongst the worthiest and the best of the King's subjects. There was also the testimony of certain hereditary enemies of the Grahams which could hardly be accepted as impartial. It will readily be seen then that, what with the overwhelming influence Cumberland could exert over the mind of King James, and the strong, one-sided evidence laid before the Council, who deemed it unnecessary to hear a word in defence of the accused, the plight of the men of Eskdale was indeed deplorable. The Grahams were not even informed of the nature of the charges laid against them, but only told, in general terms, that they were considered the worst of offenders, and, before the commission appointed to deal with the Border problem was named, a sweeping judgment was pronounced, and, by a scandalous stretch of the royal prerogative, the whole of the lands in Eskdale were confiscated and speedily conferred, by special grant, upon the favourite, Lord Cumberland.

It is interesting, in perusing these ancient documents, to follow the tone of rectitude invariably assumed by the Cumbrian gentry in those eventful times. The language of the Lawsons, the Musgraves, and others, so smacks of respectability as almost to lead to the belief that, by some mysterious freak of Providence, they, while living in the centre of Border raiding and criminal disorders, had wholly escaped the deadly evil with which the Grahams of Eskdale, in particular, were dyed black and blue. Unfortunately that supposition cannot be maintained in face of the records now in evidence, which conclusively prove that these Cumbrian gentlemen, as a class, were not better, but in some respects inferior, to the professional raider. If they no longer incurred the risk of riding in the bold foray it was not because they had become honest and reformed in character, for we find that they continued to practise incessantly the meanest of all criminal pursuits, that of the highwayman and common burglar.

Now, as it was from this class that the machinery was taken by which the Grahams of Eskdale were destroyed, it becomes interesting to know what manner of men they were.

Among the implacable foes of the Grahams were the Musgraves, whose position in Cumberland was in the front rank of landowners and magistrates, and yet we are told of warrants being out for the arrest of John Musgrave of Eden Hall, son of Sir Richard Musgrave; Thomas Hetherington, and Constable Ord, for highway robbery in Scotland. We are also told of a midnight attack upon the person of Richard Craven, deputy receiver of his Majesty's revenues in Cumberland and Westmorland. £200 were taken from him, besides his books, bills, and bonds. The thieves in this case were proved to have been Thomas, son of Sir Richard Musgrave of Morton, John Musgrave and Richard Pickering of Crosby-Ravensworth, the two last named being of the household of Sir Richard of Eden Hall. All these thieves were captured at Hexham, found to be in possession of the plunder, and were conducted to Carlisle in the custody of their near relative, Captain Musgrave.[1] But as the excuse was urged that they were *only young men*, and as there is no record of trial or punishment, it is not unreasonable to conclude that they were pardoned, as it was thought becom-

[1] *Muncaster Papers*, January 26, 1606.

ing in those days that gentlemen of quality should be.

These crimes, it may be mentioned, were committed at the very time the machinery was being organised for the crusade against the Grahams. Again, on the first of June, 1605, while Sir Wilfred Lawson was assuring the Privy Council that the county was practically free from crime, save only the misdeeds of the Grahams, a gentleman of the name of Carlton living near London, along with his Cumbrian associates, attacked Mungo Ribton, William Wichliffe, and William Stockdale, while they were travelling on the high way near Gilsland upon the affairs of the Earl of Northumberland, and not only robbed them of their horses, money, and apparel, but carried two of them away to be held to ransom in the usual brigand fashion. Not only so, but they succeeded in exacting a ransom for their freedom from these gentlemen upon a scale so extravagant as to utterly ruin the poor men's estates and families. In vain the victims petitioned the Council for redress, and equally in vain they prosecuted the matter at Carlisle. No punishment was inflicted on the criminals, who went about free from arrest, and no recompense was ever made[1]. A further instance of the extreme reluctance to put the law in motion against criminals belonging to the influential houses is that of Hugh Carlisle of Birtley, who petitioned in vain for more than nine years for the apprehension of Thomas Rotherforth of Rochester, John Rotherforth, *alias* John the Galliard, and seven others, notorious offenders who had robbed him and cut off his left hand, all of whom were allowed to go about quite openly in public[2]. It is difficult for us, accustomed as we are to the civilised conditions of modern times, to realise how perfectly appalling was the moral and the social degradation of what might be called the

[1] Ribton's Petition to the King, July 19, 1605.
[2] *Muncaster Papers*, July 13, 1605.

leading Border families in those days. What would be thought nowadays of a country gentleman and Justice of the Peace whose sons and friends (the familiar inmates of his house), spent the dark hours of night as footpads and highwaymen, the head of the house, responsible for the peace of the district, being unable to maintain the rudimentary forms of respectability and honesty within his own home? This was the class from which the machinery was chosen, be it remembered, to eradicate the accumulated evils of ages of misrule, and to lay the foundation of those necessary reforms in tune with the changed conditions of the country—commissioners taken from the very class whose reformation within their own homes was the most urgent need of the period.

Before proceeding to describe the operations of this court, composed of such strange materials, it becomes necessary to draw attention to a singular outbreak of disorder which had just occurred on the death of the Queen, historically known as the 'ill week'. The disturbances on this occasion arose from an absurd delusion which had spread among the clans that on the death of the sovereign all the laws of the land were suspended, and would so remain until the new King was proclaimed, so that during the short interregnum no malefactor could be arrested or punished for any crime, however heinous. So satisfied were the clansmen that they had now a free hand for the spoliation of their enemies, that the whole Border was soon in a blaze. The raiders flew to arms, each man burning for a final reckoning with his ancient foe. All along the frontier the battle raged, houses and strongholds were stormed and burnt, numbers of men were slain, and innumerable herds of cattle were driven in fury from place to place. No such tumult had been known on the Border for many years, and great was the alarm among the peaceable inhabitants. It was an outbreak which proved ruinous to the fortunes of the

Grahams, but a perfect god-send to the projects of Lord Cumberland, as it greatly facilitated his crusade in Eskdale by giving to the world some show of justification for the barbarous measures which were ultimately put in force. Before the sensation had subsided Lord Cumberland had begun cunningly to utilise the mischiefs of the 'ill week' by trying to prove that the Grahams of Eskdale were the only aggressors. But the Privy Council had already been flooded with reports, complaints, and petitions involving every clan on the Border in pretty equal degrees of guilt. Every fighting man of every tribe had been out, and in the mingled uproar the identification of the specially guilty was found to be hopeless. Moreover, the government was aware that a punitive invasion of the whole Border as a first taste of the effects of the Union would be highly impolitic, even had the Crown possessed the military force to deal with every clan implicated in the general outbreak of the 'ill week'. Under all the circumstances the Council wisely concluded that discretion was the better part of valour, and resolved to take a lenient view of the little misunderstanding of the law under which the clansmen were labouring during those seven memorable days devoted to the cracking of each other's crowns. A free pardon was proclaimed to all, without exception, as a special act of grace from the King on his accession to the Crown of England, and no one was to be meddled with for any act done by him during the 'ill week', a pardon which had been issued prematurely, and without consultation with Lord Cumberland, for we shall presently see how far the Grahams of Eskdale were allowed to share in its benefits.

It would be an idle task to attempt to extenuate or whitewash the offences of the Grahams or any other clan active on the Border 300 years ago. After the Union the continued existence of their customs was impossible, and it was undoubtedly the first duty of the government to deal with a state of things at variance with all the essentials of civilised life. But, in dealing with the Border chieftain, King James and his Council invariably acted upon the assumption that the whole of a community living under protection and paying blackmail were either incorrigible malefactors themselves or, being the friends and relatives of outlaws, were quite beyond the pale of civilisation, and only fit for extermination by fire and sword. No reasonable consideration was given to the fact that an evil fate, beyond their own control, had fixed their destiny in that unsettled land, and left them the heirs and inheritors of the rude methods and customs of their ancestors. The clansman only knew the rough requirements of Border laws which had come down to him from his forefathers, and no monarch or statesman had ever attempted to lay hold of his intelligence in order to teach him the advantages arising from a more settled and civilised state of existence. All the projects of reform came to the Borderer in the shape of savage raids to enforce obedience to laws wholly unknown to him, and to reduce him to starvation and misery as a first condition of orderly citizenship. This stupid practice was persisted in by both governments, in spite of its obvious failure, for many centuries, and was mainly responsible for the wild and ungovernable character of the mosstrooper, as well as the wretched moral and ecomonic condition of the Borderer at the time of the Union.

As fighting organisations they had lost the real source of their vitality when Scott of Buccleuch and Ker of Ferniehirst dissolved their bands and made their peace with the government. The time had come when many offenders, weary of their wild, precarious manner of livelihood, had taken to tillage and other decent employments, and would thankfully have accepted the protection of just laws, firmly administered, if the statesmanship of the country had been equal to the emergency.

MUNCASTER CASTLE

CHAPTER XV

COMMISSION FOR THE PACIFICATION OF THE BORDER

AMONG the many interesting manuscripts at Muncaster Castle there is a folio volume in a parchment cover fastened with an ancient clasp. It contains copies of letters and documents relating to the commission appointed by King James for the pacification of the Border, to which reference has already been made. It is believed that these copies were made for Joseph Pennington of Muncaster, one of the Commissoners, from originals in the possession of Sir Wilfred Lawson, the most active of his colleagues, and the custodian of their papers. They are all written in a small, neat hand, and are almost in chronological order. We find that, on the 25th of February, 1605, this memorable Commission was appointed and instructed by the Privy Council as to the scope of its operations. It was directed to fix its attention upon offenders of the name of Graham, no other clan being specially referred to. The directions were as follows:

'Those malefactors of the name of Graham who have been received to their submission, are not to be meddled with for any offences committed before their submission. Persons under bail to appear at the jail delivery, are to be left for trial there. All persons living within the bounds of the commission, or in certain other specified districts, are forbidden the use of all manner of armour and weapons, and of horses, "savinge meane naggs," for their tillage.

The evidence of a Scotchman against an Englishman, and of an Englishman against a Scotchman, to be received'[1].

The Commission was to consist of ten members, five English and five Scotch, with a curious, and as it proved, unworkable arrangement as to their respective authority. It was settled, to quote the instructions, as follows:

'One on the English side to be the commander of all the rest for the first three months, and another one on the Scotch side for three months, and so, afterwards, alternately. All deadly feuds are to be suppressed; fugitives from one country to the other are to be delivered to the ordinary officer on demand. All in whom there can be no hope of amendment may be removed to some other place where the change of air will make in them an exchange of their manners. All idle vagabonds to be expelled from the bounds of the commission. The armour which had served the broken people in their lewd actions, within these bounds, may be taken from them. A certificate of proceedings to be sent to the Council of both kingdoms every two months.'

The five English Commissioners were Sir Wilfred Lawson, Sir William Selby, Robert Delaval, Joseph Pennington, and Edward Grey of Morpeth. The Scotch were Sir William Seaton, Sir William Holmes, Patrick Chermiside of East Nesbit, John Charteris of Amisfield, and Gideon Murray of Elibank. The shires and towns within the bounds of their authority were Northumberland, Cumberland, Westmorland, with the parishes of Norham, the Holy Island, and Bedlington, parcel of the county palatine of Durham on the south side of the Border. On the north side there were the shiredoms and towns of Berwick, Roxburgh, Selkirk, Peebles, Dumfries, and the stewartries of Kirkcudbright and Annandale.[2]

[1] Paper dated Feb. 14, 1605.
[2] *Muncaster Papers*, Feb. 26, 1605.

It will thus be seen, both from the comprehensive instructions and the wide field of operations decided upon, that the government meant the country to understand this was to be an honest effort to solve the Border problem in its widest sense: a problem bristling with so many difficulties that only exceptionally unbiased and able men could successfully deal with it. Above all, they required to be men free from suspicion of personal interest, prejudice, or animosity in regard to individuals whose fate might rest in their hands. The question, indeed, being one of the most critical which confronted the government at the Union, called for the employment of the ablest statesmen of the period. The evil customs of centuries had to be uprooted by the exercise of patience, firmness, and discretion. The refractory clans were to be reduced to obedience, and the crop of weeds gradually eliminated, so that the ground might be prepared for the final overthrow of the ancient system and the way opened up for the introduction of settled laws. For this great purpose the Commissioners selected were all local men of the class of squireens; more or less hangers-on to Lord Cumberland, whose exalted position naturally overawed them. Besides, they were men, in many cases, entangled in the feuds and contentions of those they were called upon to judge. As might have been expected, no sooner had these Commissioners begun their deliberations than it became apparent that their entire interest was fixed upon the question of Eskdale. The large question of the settlement of the Border was hardly referred to at all; their only business seemed to lie in a zealous determination to carry out the wishes of Lord Cumberland in clearing his free grant of the dispossessed lairds and tenants. For this single purpose the whole powers of the Commission were unhesitatingly utilised, as if the installation of his lordship in his new domain was a matter of such national importance as to call for an unprecedented effort at whatever cost, in men or money, to the English government.

While these sinister preparations were on foot for crushing the Grahams the woeful tidings had reached Eskdale that they were all reduced to ruin by the act of confiscation. There was consternation and grief in every household, and probably the first impulse of the clan, in face of such injustice, would be to fly to arms, and had the strong alliances of former days been available, they would have ridden forth to defy the Crown, as in the days of old, regardless of their fate. Now resistance was hopeless against the power of both kingdoms under the direction of one supreme head. Fretting under their great sorrow, they seem quietly to have awaited the gathering storm which was soon to break upon their devoted heads. The Commission was presided over by Sir Wilfred Lawson; his colleagues were merely items who did as they were told in the execution of 'his lordship's business.' All papers addressed to the Privy Council, or to officers and agents, bore his signature, to which other names were occasionally added to save appearances. Knowing every Graham, and probably every acre of land in Eskdale, he made it his first duty to prepare a list of those whose eviction from the Cumberland grant should take precedence of all else. They were selected, not because of any definite offence that could be alleged against them, but because they were the greatest sufferers, and consequently the most dangerous and undesirable persons to be permitted to remain within sight of their old homes. It was obvious that Lord Cumberland's grant would only have been a gift of doubtful value if these ruined Grahams, hot with indignation at their wrongs, had been allowed to remain members of a community which was henceforth to acknowledge him as its lord.

It was resolved, therefore, for the comfort of his lordship, that 149 Grahams, selected by Lawson as in his opinion fit subjects for transportation, should be immediately banished to that 'somewhere' mentioned by the Privy Council 'where the change of air would make in them a change of their manners.' Among the persons named in this black list were William Graham of Mote and Arthur his brother, Richard Graham of Netherby, Richard Graham, called 'Jock's Ritchie'; John Graham, called 'All our Eames'; Hutchin Graham, known as 'Young Hutchin'; George Graham, 'Geordy's Sandie'; Richard Graham, *alias* 'Long Ritchie', and Thomas Graham of Easton[1]. All these persons were summoned to make their submission at Carlisle on a given date, without reason being assigned; and to this summons, with one or two exceptions, they appeared. Now it seems unlikely, had they been the incorrigible malefactors described by Sir Wilfred Lawson, that they would have yielded obedience so promptly to the word of authority, and it may be taken as certain that they would not have surrendered at all if they had suspected the fate awaiting them. There was a reason, however, for their peaceful submission which oozed out afterwards. Lord Cumberland had taken means to assure them that arrangements had been made to provide their wives and children with homes as good as those they were leaving in Eskdale on condition of their making prompt submission. If any such arrangement had ever been contemplated it was either unknown or disregarded by the Commissioners sitting in Carlisle.

On the surrender of the Grahams they were seized and lodged in the common gaol, and from that hour many of them never saw wife or child again.

The arrest of so large a number without the least disturbance or bloodshed was a great success, whatever may have been the stratagem employed; but, having secured them, the Commissioners were in no way prepared to deal with them. The prison was

[1] *Muncaster Papers*, April, 17, 1605.

crowded and insanitary. Nothing was fixed as to their final destiny beyond the vague instructions from the Council that they were to be removed to some unnamed region where 'the change of air would make in them a change of manners.' After much delay and great perplexity the Privy Council finally sent instructions to have them removed to Newcastle-on-Tyne, as the King had determined to banish them to Holland. England had no penal settlements in those days, but she held possession of three towns in Holland, Flushing, Brill, and Ramikins, which were known as 'the cautionary towns' from the fact that they were held as security for a loan of eight hundred thousand pounds, lent by Queen Elizabeth to assist the young republics in their war against Spain. At each of these towns there was a fortress garrisoned by English troops, under the command of Lord de Lisle, and to those Dutch stations it was decided to transport the Grahams of Eskdale.

All those fit for military service were to be incorporated with the garrisons, only with this essential disability, they were doomed to perpetual exile, and to be permanently debarred from all the privileges and freedom accorded to the regular soldiers.

By an order of Council dated May 17th, 1605, the Commissioners were informed of King James' decision, and instructed as follows: 'The King's clemency towards the Grahams who have submitted themselves has been shown in pardoning their lives and furthermore in disposing of them so that in no case shall they be in worse condition than his other good subjects who have not been offenders, being appointed to serve in the garrisons of the cautionary towns of Brill and Flushing, places where many honest men desire to be maintained in service. You are to appoint discreet persons to conduct them to Newcastle by the last day in June, whence 100 will be conveyed to Flushing and 50 to Brill. For the charges of the journey to Newcastle we require you to provide as much money as will serve them at the rate of 8d. a day to every man, and four shillings a day for each of the conductors, and the money so disbursed by you will be repaid out of the exchequer'[1].

This paper is peculiarly characteristic of the wisdom and statecraft of King James. Blind as usual to all ideas of equity and common sense, he actually claims the gratitude of his wretched victims immured in the 'pestered' gaol at Carlisle for his great clemency in having spared their lives, regardless of the fact that they were untried, unconvicted, and the great majority of them charged with no more definite offence than an unfortunate surname or the general charge of disobedience.

Of course the head and front of their offending was their presence on Lord Cumberland's grant. It does, however, seem remarkable that so few definite charges of raiding or other crimes could be found against a clan so numerous as the Grahams at this particular juncture, when no stone would be left unturned to damn them, and so justify the glaring cruelty of their treatment. The only charge of any moment was one which, having been committed in the 'ill week', was already pardoned and ought not to have been raked up. The offenders in this case were Hutchin Graham of Gards, and young Graham of Netherby, whose conduct is described as follows: '1. On Monday, after the Queen's death, he [Hutchin] neglected to stay his friends from their invasion, although admonished to do so by the Bishop of Carlisle, who saw them from the ramparts of the Castle. 2. On Tuesday following he brought one hundred and forty of his kinsmen and friends, English and Scotch, to the town of Cargo, near Carlisle, and provided them with victuals for themselves and their horses, free of cost, at the charge of the town. He had for many years taken this

[1] *Muncaster Papers*, May 17, 1605.

town into his protection, receiving from each husbandman four pecks of malt yearly for blackmail, these pecks being of Carlisle measure, 20 gallons to the bushel. 3. On the Wednesday following he crossed the Eden into Grinsdale, where he and his company as men of war erected two pensills of linen cloth on the top of lances. 4. On that day he and his company armed with jacks, spears, pistols and steel caps assaulted Captain Bowyer, his lieutenant, and his soldiers. 5. Seeing a company of the townsmen of Carlisle coming to the rescue of his Majesty's soldiers, he and his company went westwards. They spoiled a place called Bow, robbing men in the way, and afterwards spoiled the town of Orton, where they burned the house of Johnston and took prisoners. 6. He went back to Cargo, and there divided such spoil as was brought in by his company, he and young Graham of Netherby as captains taking an eighth of the whole spoil. 7. Having obtained from the King a promise of remission, he has not made restitution to the parties grieved. He has refused to go to the Low Countries and become a ringleader of nineteen others of his name who have fled into Scotland"[1]. It may be here noted that the King's pardon for the raids of the 'ill week' was unconditional. That Hutchin had made 'no restitution' was only a weak excuse for excluding the Grahams from the general pardon.

If this raid of Hutchin was the worst that could be alleged against the Grahams they do not seem to have been very deeply implicated in what was described as an unparalleled outburst of spoliation and slaughter in that memorable 'ill week.'

Transportation for life to a foreign fortress was to these Borderers a heavier doom than even the scaffold, for to them it meant not only an eternal farewell to their beloved Eskdale, but it also implied an

[1] *Muncaster Papers.* Misdemeanours of Hutchins Graham, f. 125.

extinction of every earthly interest, and the renunciation of every human tie. But apart from its flagrant injustice, it was in the highest degree impolitic to drive such men to desperation, and thus precipitate a period of bloodshed and confusion with which the feeble local Commission was wholly unfitted to deal. The King and Council acted upon the assumption that these fiery descendants of a dauntless race could be gathered together and removed from their green acres to hopeless banishment with the same quiet submission as a flock of sheep. In no long time they discovered their mistake.

On the removal of the prisoners from Carlisle gaol it was found that of the one hundred destined for Flushing seven had made their escape, and twenty-one were either dead or dying. The remaining seventy-two were conveyed to Newcastle, where they were shipped under the supervision of the Mayor, each prisoner receiving two shillings for his support for three days and beyond that—whatever provision heaven might send! The whole of their property was taken away to deprive them of the means of returning home; and so, in utter poverty, their minds torn with grief and anxiety for the fate of wives and children left plundered and starving in Eskdale, they passed away into the mists of the North Sea. Soon afterwards fifty were landed at Brill, making a total consignment of one hundred and twenty-two of the leading men of the once powerful clan banished to a spot where King James and his favourite were well satisfied that they would be heard of no more. The Council probably thought they had taken every precaution to secure their permanent exile, but in point of fact the instructions sent to Lord Lisle at Flushing were so confused and inaccurate that he altogether failed to understand that those received into the fortress were to be prisoners as well as soldiers. As to the aged and sick in a land where they knew not the language and were destitute of the means of subsistence, he simply ignored their existence.

In his report to the Privy Council on July 7th, Sir Wilfred Lawson says: 'We have sent seventy-two Grahams to Newcastle with two shillings apiece for three days, and nineteen pounds for their conductors. Of the seven principal Grahams whom we denounced as fugitives four have submitted themselves, and have gone with the others—viz., Richard Graham, son of Walter of Netherby; David Graham, of the Bankhead; Alexander Graham, of Kirkandrews, *alias* Geordy's Sandy; and Hutchin Graham of Rowcliffe. Hutchin Graham of Gards still gives out that he has a free pardon for himself and all his, whereas the King's warrant applies to five only, of whom two dwell in Scotland. One has been hanged, and one has willingly gone to Flushing. Jock of the Pear Tree is the other. We have expelled the families and uncovered the houses of those who still stand out'[1]. There is grim humour in Lawson's admission that of five holding the King's pardon one has been 'transported and one hanged.' Notwithstanding the successful opening of the campaign in Eskdale, the Commissioners ere long began to realise that their task was a great deal more serious and complicated than they had anticipated. They had by no means captured all the Grahams 'fit for transportation.' Many important men of the race had taken refuge among their friends and relations, the Maxwells and Johnstons, in Scotland, while others were believed to be harboured by Sir John Lowther. The Earl of Montrose had also come forward to protest against the arrest of his cousin of Netherby, for whose good behaviour he was willing to become security. Then came the escape of twenty-nine condemned prisoners from Carlisle gaol, which brought down words of heavy censure from the Crown as follows: 'It has been no pleasing information to his Majesty, and evil news to us,

[1] Commissioners to Lord Salisbury, July 7, 1605.

to hear of the escape of twenty-nine condemned prisoners from the gaol at Carlisle. It seems strange that you should not have told us what has become of them, or what course you have taken for their recapture.' To which Lawson replies: 'We have taken order that Sir Henry Leigh and Sir William Cranston, with the horseman in his Majesty's pay under their charge, shall go to the west parts to search for the condemned prisoners, and, if they have taken to the woods, to demolish their houses, to expel their families, and to apprehend their aiders and comforters. Forty horsemen have been enrolled for this purpose.'

With regard to the military force referred to by Lawson, it ought to be stated that government had placed at the service of the Commission two companies of horsemen, or 'horse garrisons' as they were called. One of these, under the command of Sir Henry Leigh, was stationed at Netherby, and the other, commanded by Sir William Cranston of that ilk, occupied Hollows, in Canonbie, both on the banks of the Esk. Now, as the success of the crusade mainly depended upon the friendly co-operation of these two officers, it becomes interesting to ascertain how far they agreed in regard to the duties expected of them. Sir Henry Leigh was faithfully obedient to the English Commissioners, and was prepared to strike down the undesirables in Eskdale with all his might, and soon he showed that his whole attention was fixed upon that one business. Sir William Cranston, on the other hand, felt in no way bound to obey the orders of Sir Wilfred Lawson, being officially the servant of the Scottish, not the English, Commissioners; and although quite willing to co-operate with Leigh in arresting outlaws of any clan in strict accordance with the government's instructions for the general pacification of the Border, he was not willing to join in a headlong crusade against men because of their surnames, and against whom no definite charge of crime had been alleged. In taking up this attitude it soon became apparent that he was acting with the secret concurrence of the Scotch Commissioners, who declined to support Sir Wilfred Lawson's imperious demands for the arrest of Eskdale men who had fled into Scotland, and were notoriously walking about openly in the neighbourhood of the garrison at Hollows. As may well be supposed, this state of affairs led to many angry altercations, in which the cleavage between the English and the Scotch Commissioners became daily more acute, and the national prejudices began to harden up as of old. Sir Wilfrid Lawson appealed to the Privy Council in the hope of procuring Cranston's removal as inefficient and disobedient, while Sir Henry Leigh was extolled for the activity and enterprise of his service.

The appeal to the Council, however, came too late, as Sir William Cranston had already begun to earn golden opinions from the public in general, who had been surprised and pleased with his tremendous energy and success in grapling with the irreclaimable malefactors. In the honest performance of the duty which seemed to lie before him he had scoured the Scottish side of the Border from Berwick to the Solway, capturing large numbers of the worst thieves and oppressors, and bringing them to justice at Hawick, Jedburgh, and Dumfries.

Meanwhile his English colleague, Sir Henry Leigh, was raiding and plundering among the farm-houses on Lord Cumberland's grant, assisted by one Sir William Hutton, who was accused by one of the Scottish Commissioners of arresting men and then selling them their liberty for so much hard cash.

Not even the great influence of the favourite could blind the Council and the public to the merits of the Scotch soldier and the demerits of the English. So that Lawson and his colleagues, finding it impossible to use the same tyrannical methods north of the Border which Leigh practised with freedom in the south, began to realise dangers and difficulties in clearing his lordship's grant which they had not anticipated.

Still it will be remembered the Commission was armed with supreme power to arrest, banish and hang in accordance with its own discretion.

Sir Wilfred Lawson and his colleagues were to be the sole judges as to who were offenders, who were idle vagabonds, who were those in whom no hope of amendment could be found, and above all who were those (without any reason assigned) who were to be condemned as 'fit for transportation.'

Armed with these great powers, the whole of the English marches were searched, but most of the fugitives had fled. Their houses, however, were completely destroyed, and the aged, the women, and the children left on the bare hill-sides with neither food nor shelter.

CHAPTER XVI

PROGRESS OF THE CRUSADE

IT is necessary now to revert to the fortunes of the one hundred and twenty-two Grahams banished to the cautionary towns in Holland.

The King, Cumberland, and the Commission were all profoundly satisfied with the success of that transaction. With very little trouble or expense, no public uproar or bloodshed, indeed nothing but by the employment of a little skilful treachery, Eskdale had been swept of nearly every formidable Graham —swept away, apparently for ever, to a region beyond the tempests of the North Sea.

It seemed beyond all question that by this clever stroke the Grahams had at last received their *coup de grace*, and that there now only remained the scattered and leaderless clans to be disposed of at leisure.

The possibility of their return from banishment never dawned upon the minds of their persecutors, for to all appearances such an event was impossible, because they possessed neither the means nor even the power of speech, and the facilities for ocean travel in those days were few and far between; but that they were succoured in some mysterious way is beyond doubt, otherwise a large number of them must have perished on that desolate shore of brown mud upon which they were left exposed to the storms of the Northern Ocean.

King James was made aware of their existence by a petition which they contrived to send, a petition it will be observed asking for merciful consideration for those near and dear to them. Whether his Majesty had leisure in the midst of his many amusements to read the petition is unknown, but certainly it was duly received at Whitehall. 'Many of us', they write, 'who were true men, confessed ourselves offenders by reason of the Earl of Cumberland's promise, that provision should be made for our wives and children (nearly one thousand in number) as good as that we had in Esk. We therefore pray for the fulfilment of this promise. We could in one month raise three hundred men able to serve his Majesty under our own leaders. We are ready to go to the mouth of the cannon, to the block, or to the gibbet to show our loyalty'[1]. Such a petition as this fell upon deaf ears, but soon a disquieting rumour reached Carlisle that certain well-known Eskdale men, recently transported to Holland, had been seen in Scotland, and scarcely had the Commission recovered from the shock of this incredible news than authentic tidings came to hand of the safe arrival in the Forth of sixty-one of the banished undesirables. By what agency they were not only saved from starvation, but picked up on the Dutch sands, maintained on board ship, and landed in the Forth, free of all cost, is a mystery which will probably never be solved. The most likely conjecture points to the connivance of Lord de Lisle the commandant at Flushing. When taken to task by the Council he denied having received any definite instructions to detain the Grahams as prisoners, and considered himself free to give licences to return if he chose to do so, and this he did with a readiness which is not free from suspicion.

Immediately on landing twenty-four of the Grahams boldly made for Eskdale in search of their destitute wives and children, and from that moment began that memorable struggle, so full of enormities which, but that we remember that all things were possible

[1] Petition of the Graham's to King James, *Muncaster Papers.*

under the rule of James the First, we should reject as absolutely incredible.

From a paper dated October 19th, 1605, we gather that the Council had received the news of the Grahams' return, and sent instructions accordingly. His Majesty had been made acquainted with 'the care and diligence' of the Commission in trying to sift out the manner and means of the return of the Grahams from the Low Countries. 'His pleasure is', he says, 'that all who have come with a pass shall be sent back to Newcastle to be there embarked and returned to the captain under whom they served. We have written to the Mayor of Newcastle and Viscount de Lisle, governor of Flushing. You are to proceed according to justice against those who have returned without licence, concerning their former offences, and keep them in prison until his Majesty's pleasure is known'[1].

The fugitives were to be proceeded against 'concerning their former offences.' To send them to the scaffold merely because of their return from Holland without a licence was a somewhat risky alternative, especially in view of the rising resentment of the Scotch. It was considered a safer policy to proceed by way of indictment for offences alleged to have been committed during the 'ill week' or earlier, and so completely were the ashes of the past raked up that the inhabitants of Tynedale, stirred to indignation, sent a petition to the King, in which they alleged that, among other enormities, one man was hanged for an offence committed before he was twelve years of age.

A great many were executed for their supposed connivance in the murder of Sir John Carmichael eight years earlier, whose death must have been amply avenged if all who suffered were parties to it. The death of Carmichael was really an act of vengeance on the part of the Armstrongs, in which

[1] Council to English Commissioners, Oct. 19, 1605.

the Eskdale men were in no way likely to have been concerned.

Others were hanged for having been seen where riots were raging during the 'ill week'—indeed, it was impossible for any Graham, whose death was desired, to escape the gallows. Sir Henry Leigh had little difficulty in making arrests, as many of the fugitives clung to their families until they were actually ridden down.

Meanwhile, the Scottish Commissioners were becoming daily more resentful and disinclined to assist their English colleagues in their crusade against the Grahams.

Hutchin Graham of Gards and other important Eskdale men still walked about unmolested in the neighbourhood of Hollows. Sir William Cranston's steady determination not to arrest any man against whom no reasonable charge of crime was alleged saved the lives of many, but led to incessant wrangling with Lawson. Instead of surrendering the fugitive Grahams, the Scotchmen began to demand the surrender to them of a large number of Cumbrian malefactors, many of them members of leading families, for murders and spoliations in Scotland, and for whom warrants had been issued in vain.

Sir William Cranston, finding that his station at Hollows had been fixed more with a view to crush the Grahams than as a convenient centre for operations against Border outlaws in general, removed his garrison further north without consultation. In answer to a hot remonstrance from Lawson, he explains his conduct in the following letter. 'I returned from Esk', he writes, 'because I found it unprofitable to remain there. You will find after experience that his Majesty could be better served with less stir. I was forced to admit outlaws to bond because my company was dispersed in two or three parts, and I have not the commodity of a gaol at Hollows. *After lawful advertisement* I will present such of yours as fall into my hands, or else a sufficient penalty. As for such as offended in Scotland, I await the orders of the joint commission. If you will needs be commanders, I desire that your discretion may appear as well as your authority. Think not that my body can be everywhere to do all your services. Our own courts approach. I am charged with the apprehension of the Grahams and several other duties. None come to me with armour, and for me to ride to their several homes would be an infinite travel'[1]. The removal north of Cranston was a distinct misfortune to the Eskdale fugitives, as it left the way open to military raids from Cumberland, which were forthwith organised and executed with vigour.

If Cranston remained unwilling to act against the Grahams indiscriminately, no fault could be found with Sir Henry Leigh on that score, for his entire attention was concentrated upon the clearance of the Cumberland grant. He gave the fugitives no rest, and curiously enough was allowed to carry on the campaign among the oppressed inhabitants with a steady eye to his own personal advantage. With the consent of the Commission he was allowed to appropriate to himself whatever booty came in his way. He also claimed the escheats of the goods of fugitives and their abettors, along with the whole of the forfeited recognisances, in order to assist him, as he expressed it, 'in the burden of his service.' As it was repeatedly stated that the whole cost of the military was defrayed by Government, it would be interesting to know what these burdens could be which necessitated such a very remarkable and haphazard recompense. It was enough, however, that his claim was allowed by the Privy Council, under the strong recommendation of Sir Wilfred Lawson, and thus the crusade became to Leigh a commercial enterprise of some importance. Along with Sir

[1] Cranston to English Commissioners, 1606.

Henry Leigh there was another officer, Sir William Hutton, who, if we are to believe one of his colleagues on the Scottish side of the Commission, found warrants were instruments of considerable value, which he readily but secretly turned to cash, selling men their lives practically for so much ransom as they or their friends could provide.

Meanwhile, certain grumblings were beginning to arise at the extraordinary 'deviations from humanity' in full swing throughout the Graham country. Sir Roger Wilbraham interfered to save George Graham of Burnfoot, whom he knew to be a respectable man who had done loyal service in the past, but was now lame and impotent, living quietly at his home with wife and twelve children. Sir Wilfred Lawson defended the arrest of this man on the ground that he was disobedient, inasmuch as he had failed to appear in answer to the original summons. Besides, added Lawson, George Graham was at the spoiling of Orton and the burning of Richard Johnston's house during the 'ill week.'

The Earl of Northampton, himself a lord of the Privy Council, was moved to inquire into the arrest of George and William Graham of Rose Trees, against whom nothing criminal was alleged. An inquiry from such a high quarter required a definite and satisfactory answer, but before replying to his lordship Lawson prudently advised with his agents so as to put them upon their guard. 'If the two Grahams', he wrote, 'mentioned in Lord Northampton's letter are not already transported to Brill they may be respited, otherwise, if they are gone, inquiry must be made as to their conduct during the "ill week." In other words, if the punishment has already been inflicted you must have wit enough to procure some justification for it to satisfy Lord Northampton's inquiry.'

The Duke of Lenox interested himself in William Graham of Rose Trees, and obtained permission for his return from Brill. Complications and difficulties increased on all sides. Lawson, in a state of depression, writes to Lord Cumberland telling him that he is troubled with an infirmity in his leg, but assures him that he will perform the commands given to him to the uttermost in his power if he can travel but ten miles a day. 'But', says he in despair, 'the Grahams are returning daily. If some order be not taken they will all be shortly at home again.' To the Council he writes on May 26th, 1606, 'Many of the Grahams returned from the cautionary towns, some fugitives of that name, and divers of those who broke out of Carlisle Castle remain dispersed in Eskdale, and in the adjoining counties of Scotland with desire rather to hide themselves than to do much hurt. When Sir Henry Leigh and Sir William Cranston came to garrison in Esk they withdrew themselves among the Carlyles, the Johnstons, and other families related to them. After Sir William Cranston returned to his own home many of them returned. Some thirteen of them have been arrested, and the rest have been forced to leave Esk. The people of Cumberland abhor and fear the name of Graham.

'We have required Sir William Cranston to return to his garrison at Hollows, and have given the like order to Mr. Leigh in place of his father. We have advised the Earl of Cumberland that his lands should not be farmed to the wives or friends of the Grahams. We have committed to Carlisle Gaol divers of the Grahams who have neither been offenders of late years, nor have returned from the cautionary towns. Their restraint will not a little bridle their friends who are out. We desire that offences committed in the middle shires should be exempted from pardon by special proviso'[1].

On July 30th, 1606, the Commission further report that 'Having taken very great bonds of fathers and

[1] English Commissioners to Lord Salisbury, March 20, 1606.

sons as pledges, we are persuaded that all the Grahams, seeing a resolute course taken, will no longer hazard their lives, but come in readily for transportation. At the last gaol delivery on the 28th we executed none of them, and we hope to end the business without blood.'

The arrest is also announced of Walter Graham of Netherby, William of Rose Trees, Alexander Graham, 'Bills Sandie'; Matthew Graham, *alias* 'Plump', and four others, three of whom were of the twenty-nine who broke Carlisle Castle. Complaint is also made that Sir William Cranston holds John Graham of the Pear Tree under arrest, but refrains from sending him to Carlisle as directed, 'though he is a notable thief, none worse'[1], and Sir William is further blamed that of the forty Grahams demanded of him not one has been sent to the Carlisle Gaol delivery. Cranston replies that he is sorry Lawson has again complained of him to the Council for having released some of the Grahams on their bonds, but if he likes to attend on the 17th of the month he will hear his defence of his conduct before the Council.

While frantic efforts were being made to secure the Graham fugitives hiding in Scotland, the Scottish Commissioners were as persistently clamouring for the surrender to them of a large number of Cumbrians for whom warrants were out for pillage and slaughter in Scotland. There were strong reasons for the shelter of these malefactors which gradually came to light. Many of them were employed as agents and constables in the service of the Earl of Cumberland in helping forward the evictions of the Grahams, and others were closely related to the leading families. Among these criminals was one William Taylor, a burglar of note accused of many crimes in Scotland, and whose case is typical not only of the *impartial* administration of justice under King James, but of

[1] English Commissioners to Lord Salisbury, March 20, 1606.

the lordly independence of all legal restraint in which Lord Cumberland was permitted to indulge.

When the charges against Taylor were formulated and his arrest demanded, Lord Cumberland made no attempt to deny or excuse the crimes, but finding it inconvenient to part with the service of so suitable an agent, he was able to suspend the operation of the criminal law by little more than the expression of a wish. 'Taylor', he says, 'has been employed in his Majesty's service, and has deserved well therein, especially in the taking of Roberts Sandie, a notable thief and murderer, who was present at the murder of Sir John Carmichael. Besides, Taylor had the promise of a pardon from the Bishop of Carlisle and Sir Charles Hailes'[1]. Thus an *avowed* criminal who has assisted in the capture of a *possible* criminal on the other side of the Border has purchased, by that meritorious deed a complete remission for all the burglaries and murders of which he is accused, with the Episcopal blessing added thereto.

Another case of shelter was that of Thomas Hetherington, against whom the Scotch were endeavouring to execute a warrant for murder and robbery. He had assassinated Hector Armstrong while engaged in pillaging his house at Tweden.

The defence of this malefactor was left to Sir William Hutton: 'I hear', he says, 'that a warrant has been issued to apprehend Thomas Hetherington for the killing of Hector Armstrong of Tweden. The killing of him was the best service done for the Borders of England for these twenty years, for he was a principal murderer, a great and common thief, a spoiler, and leader of the rest. If the Commissioners of Scotland shall so earnestly seek redress for such a notorious thief, what good shall we expect of them?

'The poor man Hetherington is marvellously

---

[1] Warrant from Lord Cumberland, May 23, 1605.

frightened with fear to enter into Scotland, and Lord Cumberland's business is thereby left undone'[1].

Of course all this violent denunciation of each other as murderers, spoilers and thieves was only the ordinary foul-tongued abuse of the time, the strongest vituperation usually falling from the lips of the greatest offenders. A more serious demand was urged by the Scottish Commissioners for the arrest and delivery to them of John Musgrave of Eden Hall, William Musgrave of the Castle, and their accomplices, numbering forty-eight in all, against whom there were many charges of spoliation and murder in Scotland[2]. The surrender of these malefactors was refused by the English Commissioners for reasons not more convincing than those cited above. They replied to the Scotch demand as follows: 'In the roll of names of such as you desire to be sent to Dumfries and Jedburgh are those of men of good quality, free from suspicion of theft. The matters alleged against them were done under the government of Lord Cumberland by command of his officers. We are enjoined by the Privy Council to forbear to call such to account'[3].

It will be observed that the Commissioners declared these worthies, in one sentence, incapable of the crimes, and in the next they coolly admit that they were done by order of Cumberland's agents, and were thus legalised outrages. The order from the Privy Council was clear and express, namely that all actions done by the Agents of the Earl of Cumberland were to pass without interference, 'because', it was added 'the Earl of Cumberland has deserved well of the King.'

Now it seems difficult to imagine that the Grahams of Eskdale could be guilty of any crimes more

[1] Sir W. Hutton to Sir W. Lawson, April 3, 1606.
[2] Scotch Commissioners to English Commissioners, April 19, 1606.
[3] *Muncaster Papers.*

heinous than murder and pillage, which we find here expressly condoned, if not encouraged, by his Majesty's Privy Council when perpetrated by the banditti employed by Lord Cumberland in clearing his grant of the dispossessed. While these Cumbrian malefactors were prowling about free from arrest, the unfortunate dwellers on the Cumberland grant were being executed without mercy for disobedience to a summons, or for crimes, some of which were alleged to have been committed in childhood.

CHAPTER XVII

BORDERERS SUSPECTED OF TREASON

WHILE the disputes regarding the surrender of malefactors were in full swing between the northern and southern Commissioners there occurred an event which sent a wave of consternation throughout the whole kingdom. Upon the Borderland it fell with peculiar significance, being fraught with perilous consequences to several persons of importance with whom we are concerned. This was the discovery of the memorable gunpowder plot, the historical details of which are too well known for recapitulation further than as showing how that notable event compromised the loyalty of the great Lord Northumberland, involving his agent, Sir Wilfred Lawson, in the gravest suspicion. It will be remembered that one of the chief conspirators in the plot was Thomas Percy, Lord Northumberland's near relative and the tenant of his ancient residence, Prudhoe Castle. The Percys as Papists had suffered many intolerable wrongs from the rigorous application of the penal laws which were being enforced with even greater severity under James than they had been under Elizabeth. The Catholics had expected considerable relaxation of those laws on the accession of King James because of his mother, Mary Queen of Scots, whose life the Catholics believed was sacrificed to their cause, and because James had shown decided leanings towards them in his youth. They were thus exasperated beyond measure when they discovered that the King was absolutely relentless in the severity with which he enforced the penalties enacted against them, more particularly when they saw that those enactments were turned into a source of exorbitant profit. The fines imposed were so ruinous as to reduce many families of moderate incomes to absolute beggary. But more intolerable still were the objects to which these large fines were devoted.

James, as we have seen, was surrounded by numbers of his impecunious countrymen whose habits were extravagant and whose importunities were incessant. To satisfy the more clamorous of his threadbare countrymen, who had the flagrant indiscretion to transfer to them his claims on many of the higher class of recusants, with full power to proceed by law in his name, unless the sufferers would agree to compound by the grant of an annuity for life to his Scotch pursuer or by the payment down to him of a large sum. Had these enormous fines gone to the Royal Treasury the recusants would have had good reason to complain, but that law-abiding loyal subjects should be shorn of their means to support the expenses of the King's Scottish minions aggravated their wrath and goaded even the gentlest among them to a state of desperation. Among these victims was a gentleman of position — Mr. Robert Catesby — who first conceived the idea of resorting to an unprecedented method of revenge which he divulged to his friend Thomas Percy, who at once joined him in his plot.

Catesby argued that to kill the King would be fruitless, as he had children who would succeed to his throne. Then there were ministers, parliament, and all the machinery of government infected with the same persecuting spirit, leaving no alternative but to destroy the whole at one blow. They determined, therefore, to blow up the King, the Royal Family, Lords and Commons, with all the machinery of government, in one appalling ruin. A house adjoining the Palace of Westminster was hired by Thomas Percy in the spring of 1604. Thirty-six barrels of gunpowder were successfully lodged in the vaults below the House of Lords, and all was in readiness for the approaching opening of Parliament when a suspicious looking person called Fawkes was arrested and examined, and, ultimately, being brought face to face with the rack, made a full discovery of all the conspirators. In the north country the sensation was extreme, for the great Lord Northumberland and all his adherents, prominent among whom was his agent, Sir Wilfred Lawson, fell under a cloud of suspicion.

A suspicion so grave that for a time Lord Cumberland's business in Eskdale was somewhat neglected, and the women and children upon his grant had a respite from their tormentors. Sir Wilfred Lawson had little time now to think of bad legs and other infirmities in face of the alarming probability that his patron's ruin would involve his own. His close association with the Percys for many years might now prove his destruction. He deemed it urgent, therefore, to lose no time in making an ostentatious parade of his loyalty by rushing off in search of evidence of the guilt of his former patron, and thus show his zeal in furthering the interests of justice. The alarming news reached him on his way to Newcastle, and forthwith he bent his steps towards Prudhoe, in the hope that, by a skilful arrest or the discovery of treasonable papers, he might put all question of his loyalty at rest in the mind of King James. In any case his zealous activity in searching Prudhoe without an hour's delay could not but create a favourable impression in high quarters. From Prudhoe Castle, therefore, he addressed the following letter to Lord Salisbury signed by himself and Sir William Selby.

'On Sunday the tenth instant, on our way from Carlisle to Newcastle, we heard of the horrible and graceless conspiracy against the King and the whole state. Knowing that William Ord, a pensioner of twenty pence per day, in Berwick, had the keeping of the Earl of Northumberland's castle of Prudhoe (having been preferred to that place by Thomas Percy the traitor) and become a recusant, we thought good to search the castle before going to Newcastle. We found none there except servants; Ord had left on the previous day. He was as likely as any to conceal the said Percy. There is not a more suspicious place in this country. We learned that Percy was there only a fortnight before'[1].

It behoved Lawson to parade his loyalty, for his position was one of extreme danger at that moment, when the enraged government was likely to wreak indiscriminate vengeance, not only on the conspirators but upon all their adherents. There was no man in the north of England a more conspicuous retainer of the deeply implicated house of Percy than Sir Wilfred Lawson. To the Percys he was indebted for his position, part of his income, probably his knighthood, and many advantageous preferments. If he were now to be denounced as privy to the most diabolical plot on record, no one knew better than Lawson how savage, indiscriminate and merciless would be the vengeance of King James. Moreover it would be difficult to say what adverse criticisms might arise from the voluminous correspondence, stretching over many years, while he acted as Lord Northumberland's agent. In short, there was no alternative left but to join the hue and cry against his old benefactors, boldly to seek to prove their guilt, and hunt them to destruction. In his desperate zeal to please King James he took measures to intercept the Earl of Northumberland's letters, at the Newcastle post office. These he forwarded to the Privy Council with a letter stating that the Commissioners sitting

[1] *Muncaster Papers*, Sir W. Lawson to Lord Salisbury, Nov. 12, 1605.

at Carlisle felt it their duty to take this step after grave conference together. 'So that if the said Earl be in his Majesty's good favour, the letters may be delivered to him, otherwise they may be disposed of as seems best to you.'

In spite, however, of these strenuous efforts to show his devotion to the Crown, Lawson had good reason for alarm when he was informed that a warrant had arrived from Whitehall directing Sir Henry Widderington to seize, in the King's name, the castles of Alnwick, Tynemouth, and Cockermouth, as belonging to the Percys or their adherents. Lawson himself was not only a lifelong adherent, but was the actual custodian of Cockermouth, a circumstance not unlikely to weigh heavily to his disadvantage in the eyes of men thirsting for vengeance and prone to arrive at decisions without very scrupulous regard to actual facts established by evidence. In this serious dilemma he again addressed himself to Lord Salisbury, the one strong and experienced minister who at that juncture had not lost his head and might give his case a patient hearing.

'I have heard', he writes, 'of a warrant directed to Sir Henry Widderington by the lords of the Privy Council authorising him to take into his hands the castles of Alnwick, Tynemouth, and Cockermouth, in the county of Northumberland, as being in the custody of Thomas Percy, the traitor, or his adherents. The matter of Cockermouth is mistaken. It is in the south-west part of Cumberland, nearly forty miles from any part of Northumberland, and is in my custody, who, I trust, shall never be so far destitute of God's grace as to become an adherent of that vile traitor. The castle itself is for the most part ruinous. My wife's son dwells in the gatehouse by my direction. About fourteen years since the Earl of Northumberland made me lieutenant of the Honour of Cockermouth, with a fee of £10. With this office I have the keeping of the castle, which is situated within two miles of my house. The dispossessing me of this castle, which is of small moment either of offence or defence, will breed in the heads of the people an opinion that some suspicion is held of my loyalty, and disgrace me in the government of these parts'[1].

This plausible letter failed to elicit a satisfactory response, and it was evident the government was in no hurry to accept his protestations of loyalty, or to alter the decision regarding the seizure of Cockermouth Castle, preparations for which Widderington had already set on foot.

Another appeal was made to Lord Salisbury to endeavour to dispel doubts which might still linger in his mind. In a long letter he ends by assuring him, to quote his exact words, that 'Since Thomas Percy became a Papist he has not cared to converse but with men of his own quality and others, of a better religion, have not been desirous to have much to do with him. He has not commonly resorted hither save at the times of the Earl of Northumberland's audit'[2]. Lawson thus endeavours to make Salisbury believe that Percy's change of faith closed their cordial intimacy which of late had been merely official. Hearing no favourable response to his further appeal, Sir Wilfred seems to have become despondent and prepared for the worst. Writing to his bailiff—Christopher Irton—he says, 'You will do well to send your wife and children away, and to remain at Cockermouth Castle until the coming of Sir Henry Widderington, who will put you forth, and put others in. We must obey the warrant from the lords of the Privy Council'.[3]

An official announcement had just been received

[1] Sir W. Lawson to Lord Salisbury, Nov. 14, 1605, *Muncaster Papers*.
[2] *Ibid.*, Nov. 16, 1605, *Muncaster Papers*.
[3] Sir W. Lawson to Chris. Irton, Nov. 16, 1605.

from Sir Henry Widderington of the appointment of his cousin, Mr. Carnoby, who would enter Cockermouth Castle for his Majesty, and place such persons there as he should think fit.

The widespread belief that the Popish plot had been hatched originally at Prudhoe Castle threw the whole of the Border country into a fever of excitement and speculation regarding the great persons likely to be involved. It was rumoured that Percy had fled to the north, and all magistrates and officials, civil and military, were warned to be on the watch, while the hue and cry rang through the land. Later came the news, however, that Catesby and Percy had been overtaken and shot somewhere in Worcestershire. Many of their confederates and others, in no way concerned beyond the fact that they were leading Papists, were tried and executed. Many were fined enormous sums, among them Lord Mordaunt who had to pay ten thousand pounds, Lord Stourton four thousand pounds, and the Earl of Northumberland was not only fined thirty thousand pounds, but lodged a prisoner in the Tower where he spent most of the remainder of his life. With Sir Wilfred Lawson the gloomy clouds began to dispel as the sensation subsided. Probably his close association with Lord Cumberland, the favourite, worked to his advantage, for soon he had the satisfaction of hearing from Sir Henry Widderington, who wrote from Bothel on November 24th, 1605, as follows:

'I have received letters from the Council desiring that I should forbear to seize or enter Cockermouth Castle, and that it should continue in your keeping. You know that I have not been forward or hasty in this matter'[1].

[1] Sir H. Widderington to Sir W. Lawson, Nov. 23, 1605.

CHAPTER XVIII

THE BISHOP OF CARLISLE

SIR WILFRED LAWSON'S loyalty being no longer in question he was again able to devote his entire attention to the business of Lord Cumberland, by renewing the interrupted crusade against the objectionable people of Eskdale. But another event was impending, fraught with perils and perplexities wholly unexpected.

Throughout the period of national uproar, caused by the discovery of the plot, Lord Cumberland had been confined to his bed, so dangerously ill that he had been unable to interest himself with the King for his friends in the north. He was doomed never to set foot again upon his free grant or to enjoy the fruits of his ill-gotten acquisition in Eskdale, for his disease terminated fatally. While basking in the royal favour and heaping up his earthly treasures with cynical indifference to the cost in human misery, he was called away to the final reckoning of his own last account. Lawson received the news of his death in a letter from his brother and successor to the title and estates in the following words: 'God has called my lord my brother out of this vale of misery and you have lost an honoured friend. My brother passed his estate in Cumberland to the Earl of Salisbury, myself and others. The King has granted Carlisle Castle to me for my life and the life of my son which you know my brother wished'[1].

The limits of Lord Cumberland's grant, having

[1] *Muncaster Papers*, Lord Cumberland to Sir W. Lawson, Dec. 20, 1605.

been vaguely defined, the new lord at once assumed that the King intended his late favourite to use his own discretion in the delimitation of his boundaries, and, judging from the arbitrary enclosures already made, he seems to have been justified in the assumption. Under this impression, and believing himself entitled to the unprecedented privileges of his late brother, he speedily mustered his agents and constables, gave orders to the military, and began the staking out of his lands upon a scale undreamt of even by King James. In the busy work of enclosing and appropriating, the people's ancient landmarks were treated with no more respect than if they had been chance drifts of melting snow.

Among other desirable properties he had seized the estate of Brackenhill, near Nicol forest, belonging to the widow of Richard Graham, who indignantly protested, and, producing her title deeds, showed how the property had been purchased by the father of her late husband from Sir Thomas Dacre. As it was clear the widow could not be accused either of raiding in the 'ill week', or of disobedience, the Council, to his lordship's surprise, reserved the case for consideration. Other similar claims to land in Bewcastle were also postponed for closer investigation.

Such reservations and checks were unknown in the first lord's time, and came as gentle warnings to the second, that he had not succeeded to the unquestioning supremacy of his great brother; nor were Lawson and his colleagues slow to note these ominous signs that the imperious methods of the late Earl could no longer be practised with absolute impunity by his successor. The arrests and executions for disobedience still continued, but signs were not wanting that the Privy Council had, at last, begun to realise the hopeless incompetence of the Commission to settle affairs in Eskdale, far less to deal with the larger problem of the whole Border, for which they were ostensibly appointed.

It was determined, therefore, to add to the Commission an adviser of greater force and intelligence in the person of one who had already bestirred himself somewhat actively in the interest of his friend Lord Cumberland, and who, from his sacred calling, would be likely to import a little moderation and respectability into the counsels of the Commission.

This was the Lord Bishop of Carlisle, a self-willed and masterful spirit, much more of a politician than a priest, who, from his intimacy with Cumberland, was a declared enemy of the Grahams. He was also a strong believer in the efficacy of capital punishment for the crime of disobedience. The poor people of Eskdale had nothing to hope for from the piety of the Bishop, who, far from using his influence on the side of mercy, urged the application of the death penalty with greater ferocity than any of his colleagues. The appointment of the Bishop was made at a moment when the rigour of the crusade was beginning slightly to abate, chiefly because of the King's diminished interest in the grant now that his favourite was dead, and when the addition of a humane and just Commissioner might have done much to lessen the cowardly torture inflicted not only upon disobedient men but upon the helpless widows and children.

The coming of the Lord Bishop, far from moderating, stirred afresh the flames of persecution, and on no occasion do we find his voice raised on the side of mercy. It must be said in his favour, however, that, though eager to clear the Grahams out of Eskdale, he drew the attention of his colleagues to the larger question of general pacification which all along they had practically ignored. As a loyal Cumbrian the Bishop was a marvellous expert in finding excuses for the crimes committed by his own countrymen, but had no mercy upon the northern raiders who fell into his hands. 'I took great comfort', he writes, 'to hear of the good justice done at the late jail deliveries at Newcastle and Carlisle' the phrase 'good justice' meaning the large number hanged. Still the Bishop had the merit of directing the attention of the Commission to the work for which they were appointed, and had he been able to act impartially against malefactors from both countries, his business-like energy would, in all probability, have given a death blow to the incorrigibles.

But although we find him busily concocting plans against the clansmen of Liddesdale, breathing vengeance against Whitehaugh, procuring the arrest of 'Geordie' of the Glinzier, *alias* 'Henharrow', and others, he persistently ignored the depredations of the Cumbrians. The Forsters, Taylors, and Musgraves could do no wrong.

The most serious invasions of Cumberland were carried out at this time by Armstrong of Whitehaugh, the worthy descendant of a race of brigands whose well-trained bands infested the whole of the district bordering upon Bewcastle, from which it is divided by the river Liddel.

The invasions of Whitehaugh and his allies were so incessant and ruinous that it was found necessary to establish a regular military station in Bewcastle for the defence of Cumberland. The command of this garrison was entrusted to Thomas Musgrave, who was styled Captain of Bewcastle, a gentleman in every respect typical of the race to which he belonged.

This astute officer had not been long installed as conservator of the peace in that lively district when he began to consider seriously which side promised the greatest profits to himself. On the whole the advantages seemed to lie on the side of an alliance with Whitehaugh. He thereupon deliberately arranged to facilitate, rather than check, the spoliation of his Cumbrian friends as they soon found to their cost, for never before had more valuable herds of English cattle passed unhindered through Bewcastle on their way to Liddesdale.

That the Commissioners strongly suspected the treachery of Musgrave appears from a paper addressed to the Council and signed by the Bishop of Carlisle, 'The Captain of Bewcastle', he writes, 'readily undertakes the apprehension of offenders within that charge, but he slenderly performs it. How he stood affected by the good of the country may be gathered by his affinity, in that he matched one of his base-born daughters with that bloody and thievish clan of the Armstrongs of Whitehaugh in Liddesdale, by whom, and their allies, many spoils and murders have been committed. His house has been known as an usual receptacle of these infamous sons of Sandie's Rynion, the murderers of Sir John Carmichael'[1].

Notwithstanding this plain expression of distrust of the character and conduct of an officer upon whose fidelity the lives and property of the community largely depended, addressed by his Majesty's Commissioners to his Majesty's Privy Council, no serious consequences followed. The government probably knew that Musgrave was only a fair type of the officers usually employed, and that as there was little likelihood of replacing him by a better man, he was left to continue his lucrative arrangement with his friend and relative in Liddesdale.

Complaints and remonstrances poured in from the numerous victims of Whitehaugh's activity, but the captain remained at his post little disturbed by either reproaches or threats. A feeble reprimand came from the Privy Council at times, of which the following may be quoted as an example: 'You may call the Captain of Bewcastle before you', they write, 'and tell him it is not the King's pleasure that he should by himself command all the inhabitants within that precinct, and that he must not interrupt the execution of your warrants'[2].

[1] *Muncaster Papers*, Commissioners to the Council, Nov. 22, 1606.
[2] Council to the Commissioners, Dec. 24, 1606.

The government was helpless in the rule of even its smallest officials, for in point of fact all those on the Border had the instincts of raiders, were the descendants of raiders, and could not be made to yield implicit obedience to any central authority. When employed by the government they could never recognise a limit to their powers, holding life and property at their own disposal, and so they became, to all intents and purposes, ordinary raiders armed with a license.

No place in Cumberland was more exposed to the enterprise of Armstrong of Whitehaugh than Nawarth Castle, with its fertile grass lands and tempting herds lying just beyond what Armstrong might call his buffer state of Bewcastle. It chanced that the owner —Lord William Howard, the famous 'Belted Will'— knew how to defend his possessions with as much skill and courage as any raider of the Armstrong breed. What he lost he knew how to recover, usually with considerable interest, and without being over scrupulous at whose expense the balance of the account was squared up. Indeed, life at Nawarth Castle in those days must have been impossible to any one who declined to accept frankly the conditions and play the game of plunder and reprisal like his neighbours. The danger and excitement of the foray were not without attractions to Lord William's warlike spirit. In one of his complaints to the Commissioners, however, he seems to have been somewhat down in his luck, for he says: 'Both England and Scotland "lie onelie upon me", for there is not a week, and scarce a night, but they steal either from me or my tenants. It grieves me that so wicked a thief as Flaughtaile should be transported without answering the law. Pardons have not hitherto been so easily obtained. I can prove that Archibald M'Wittie, a Scotchman, dwelling with Herbert Maxwell under Lord Maxwell, has stolen my cattle. I pray for his delivery, and that of

Archibald Armstrong, brother of Andrew of Whitehaugh, at whose house five of my cattle were found yesterday. If such felonies escape unpunished, lamentable would be the state of these parts'[1]. It would be interesting to know the circumstances under which the cattle above referred to were found at Armstrong's house, and whether the troopers who found them were scrupulously careful to lift only those which they so readily identified. The Howards were not so accurate in their cattle transactions that evidence on the other side might be safely ignored, and it is by no means unlikely that Armstrong's way of reckoning up the figures might have shown a fairly reasonable balance of accounts between himself and Lord William. We find from a series of letters which Lord William Howard addressed to Lawson, with what zest he joined in the Border fray, and with what relish he ran the Scotch marauder to earth. He describes his gallop at the heels of Thomas Armstrong, *alias* 'Edward's Tom'; of his hunt after John Armstrong, *alias* 'Jock Stow Lugs'; and Christopher Urwin, whom he pursued, riding all night with his servants and followers, chasing them to the confines of Yorkshire.

'I have been away fishing', he says, 'and took as many as I could get. I was in hopes to have taken Anton's Edward himself, but for want of a better was glad to take his son Thomas and Jock Stow Lugs, the last but not the least in villainy. I desire you to keep him as a jewel of high price. Pray cause the records to be searched. If you find matter sufficient to hang the two, hold up your finger and they shall be delivered. I confess myself a southern novice'[2]. The search of the records seems to have proved successful, for we find at the gaol delivery a fortnight later Stow Lugs, Edward's Tom, Christopher Urwin, and the 'wicked thief, Flaughtaile', were all

[1] *Muncaster Papers*, Howard to Lawson, Sept. 9, 1606.
[2] *Muncaster Papers*, Howard to Lawson, Jan. 9, 1606.

NAWORTH CASTLE

hanged. Along with these malefactors perished one John Graham for the crime of disobedience. Flaughtaile had been captured by Lord William in the bishopric of Durham, and so energetic and victorious was he over the Liddesdale limmers that the Commissioners felt bound to draw the special attention of the Privy Council to his merits in furthering the ends of justice. Under the bouyant and forcible individuality of the Lord Bishop the work of the Commission sensibly widened in its scope, but the severities in Eskdale continued, chiefly by reason of Lawson and his colleagues having gone too far to be able to retreat with safety to themselves within the lines of moderation. They had proceeded from one excess to another until the crusade had reached a point when the dangers of cunningly devised schemes of vengeance became disturbing. Around them were scores of the maddened kindred of the dead, and while such men were at large no Commissioner could sleep in peace or move about free from the dread of an encounter with a father or son of those whom he had doomed to the scaffold. It was probably terror, therefore, which drove the Commission headlong to the perpetration of such enormities that petitions for mercy began to reach the Privy Council from indignant dwellers at a distance. These signs of public resentment so troubled the minds of King James and his Council, that they discreetly sought to shift the responsibility from themselves by fixing the blame upon the backs of their incapable instruments sitting at Carlisle. 'You have been using', wrote the Council, 'more severe and "straite proceedinges" than was intended by the King by taking into question offences done upon the Border many years ago. One Michael Davidson was condemned in January last for certain felonies committed twelve years ago, when he was but twelve years of age, and a cousin of his was executed for the same offence. We cannot but be doubtful of your due observation of his Majesty's meaning'[1]. James pretended to be shocked at these outrages, although he knew that he was himself the author of the whole catalogue of horrors which had disgraced the Border towns. He knew that he had ordered the monstrous punishment of death merely for disobedience to a summons, even in cases where obedience was not within human possibility. James and his Council must have well remembered the order of June 2nd, 1605, directing that 'whosoever of the men appointed to go to the cautionary towns shall run away, shall be punished by death.' Nor could James have forgotten that he had expressly withdrawn from the Grahams the general pardon for offences of the 'ill week' in order to rake up cases against them by way of justifying in the eyes of the world the long list of confiscations, banishments, and executions.

Both King and Council were in receipt of regular reports from Lawson and his colleagues of all the arrests, condemnations, and deaths, and in no case is there to be found a syllable of remonstrance against the most obviously unjust killing of men until the voice of the public was heard.

The Commissioners seem to have put a true value upon the royal expostulation, which they knew was a piece of pure hypocrisy intended for public consumption, but not really meant to check those methods of barbarism by which alone the remainder of the Grahams could be cleared out of Eskdale.

The public interest having ceased, no change was made on the side of mercy. Scandalous punishments were duly reported, apparently to the satisfaction of James and his Council. The Grahams still at large, though greatly reduced in number, were not entirely inactive. Many of Lord Cumberland's new tenantry found their holdings in Eskdale only precarious bargains from the uncomfortable possibilities of fire

[1] *Muncaster Papers*, Council to Commissioners, March 11, 1606.

and sword, and the frequent attacks and the obstacles thrown in their way by the former tenants and friends of the dispossessed. Rob's Fergie waylaid Leigh and his attendants on the highway between Dumfries and Milleys, one of whom he shot in the ribs, captured his mare, and galloped off. At the same time Rob of Medopp was gallantly rescued from the custody of the soldiers, and many other indications of a resolve on the part of the remaining few to die fighting drove Sir Wilfred Lawson to despair.

He had now recourse to another weapon, intended to somewhat lighten his deeds in the eyes of the world. He sought to draw down upon the men of Eskdale the scorn and contempt of the world by a plan which was ingenious, but so blunderingly executed, that none could be deceived. This new device was the publication of a document alleged to be a voluntary petition from Walter Graham of Netherby and seventy-eight of his clan, addressed to King James, confessing themselves the veriest scum of the human race. It ran as follows: 'We and others, after the death of the late Queen, disorderly and tumultuously assembled with all the warlike force and power that we could, and invaded the inland part of the eastern side of Cumberland, and spoiled many Englishmen with fire and sword, robbery and murder. Some among us of evil judgment had persuaded us that until your Majesty was a crowned King of England the laws of the kingdom ceased and were of no force, and that all offences done in the meantime were not punishable. We have deserved death and the confiscation of all our lands and goods. Many of us have wives and children who may be able with better education to do good service to your Majesty in some other part of your dominions. We therefore pray that we may be relegated and banished as an evil colony to some other part of your kingdom, there to spend the remainder of our lives in sorrowing for our offences'[1].

It is instructive to note that this pretended petition is an exact summary of the oft-repeated charges made by Lawson against the Grahams, and expressed in his own peculiar phraseology. He asks the world to believe that Walter of Netherby and seventy-eight of his clan have not only been suddenly stricken to the earth with remorse for their evil lives, but in the voluntary outpourings of their penitent hearts they have, in some miraculous way, been inspired to use the very words habitual to himself. That Walter Graham of Netherby and his kindred should voluntarily confess themselves too degraded to live in a country peopled with Musgraves, Taylors, Forsters, and even Lawsons, to say nothing of Armstrongs and Maxwells, and to implore banishment as an evil colony at the moment when they were facing starvation and death rather than leave the homes of their fathers, is not only at variance with common sense, but is in direct conflict with every utterance which had hitherto fallen from their lips. They are represented as begging a king, whom they feared and detested, to inflict upon them the punishment they most abhorred for the offences of the 'ill week', against the raking up of which they had never ceased to protest. Further, one wonders where and when those seventy-eight Grahams had the opportunity of meeting to discuss and settle the terms of this extraordinary petition. Walter of Netherby was certainly in Carlisle Castle, but most of the others were either hiding in the woods to avoid the attention of Leigh's dragoons or were sheltered among the Maxwells and the Johnstons. The petition, therefore, was a complete imposture, and yet there seems to have been a small grain of foundation for the wish on the part of many of the clan to be removed from Eskdale which probably

[1] *Muncaster Papers*, Petition to the King, Aug. 14, 1606.

suggested the monstrous misrepresentation put forward by Lawson. Many of the clan, wearied with the endless oppression, and finding themselves daily exposed to the brutalities of the Musgraves, Taylors, and other agents of Lord Cumberland, resolved to ask the Commissioners to remove them, they cared not whither, but away from the hell upon earth into which Eskdale had now been converted. Upon the strength of this pathetic appeal, from a small number, Lawson built up, and issued as genuine, his foul calumny in the form of a voluntary petition. It must be remembered that the conditions of the time were such that whatever Lawson and his colleagues chose to promulgate remained unanswered. Their victims had no means of reply, no power of appeal to their countrymen for redress, and the most bare-faced falsehoods easily passed current as unanswerable truths because the victims thereof remained silent.

When the prayer for removal was beginning to be heard in Eskdale, there yet remained many who were resolved to die rather than quit their homes, and among these the foremost, and most formidable leader was Hutchin Graham of Gards already referred to, and described as the man of the greatest mind and means in the clan. His position was peculiar inasmuch as he held a special pardon for all his transgressions; a favour which arose out of the old exploit at Carlisle Castle when, in alliance with Scott of Buccleuch he rescued Kinmont Willie to the dismay and humiliation of Lord Scrope. No event during his reign in Scotland had so tickled the fancy of King James as that notable enterprise which caused him to explode in peals of laughter loud and long. He loved Buccleuch and hated Scrope, whose wardenship of the English western marches had been peculiarly unfriendly and disrespectful to himself, and he was not sorry to see Elizabeth's great Border fortress broken, and the overbearing Warden disgraced by a Border reiver and the members of his clan.

Since those days all the conditions had been changed, Elizabeth was in her grave, James of Scotland sat upon her throne, and Scott, the stark raider of other days was his confidential friend and among the best of his advisers.

What must have been the feelings of the King and Scott when they read the report from Sir Wilfred Lawson of the proceedings taken against that wicked spoiler Hutchin Graham for the offence 'of breaking into Carlisle Castle in company with the Lord of Buccleuch and other Scotchmen for the fetching of one William of Kinmont forth therefrom'[1]. Lawson, having permission to rake up the old transgressions against the Eskdale clan, had, indiscreetly, utilised this famous escapade as the most notable crime he could urge to secure a conviction against the irrepressible Hutchin. The verdict of guilty in such a case would, by all the rules of common sense, include both Scott and the King.

The wildest whimsicalities of the comic opera were never more flagrant than the ordinary daily events of administration in the reign of King James. George Meredith has somewhere described the great human procession marching blindly on amidst the unheard derisive laughter of the gods, and one might add that the deities of Olympus must have had some uproarious hours of entertainment watching the performances of the great Jove of England. We are unable to trace the ultimate fate of Hutchin Graham but may charitably conclude that Scott would save him from the scaffold at least, but so long as he remained at liberty in Canonbie he inspired so much hope and courage among his brother fugitives, and was so notoriously favoured by Sir William Cranston that the English Commissioners resolved to cross the Border and scour the Canonbie district

[1] *Muncaster Papers*, f. 66.

with their own Cumbrian forces. The invasion of Canonbie was a risky expedient in the then temper of the Scotch, but the exasperating impartiality of Sir William Cranston in declining to arrest Grahams against whom no definite charge of crime was alleged; his utter indifference to the interests of Lord Cumberland and his general unwillingness to assist in the Eskdale crusade, seem to have left the Commissioners no alternative but to run down the required disobedients with their own superior forces. The command of the horsemen selected for this purpose was given to John Musgrave of Plumpton who forthwith crossed the Border at the head of twenty men. He marched direct north by way of Glenzier Burn, Overtown, and Glenzier Head, his object being to reach Barngleese, the abode of Christopher Armstrong the laird, a man of means, and highly popular along the Borderland. Whatever the laird may have been in his younger days, he was now too old to be personally concerned in any of the aggressive disorders of the time, and as his lands were far beyond the limits of the Cumberland grant Musgrave could have no reason for an attack on Barngleese save for plunder. He came, therefore, as a licensed freebooter and with his twenty men broke into the laird's house in the dead of night. Having plundered the old man of his money and belongings, and probably thinking that dead men tell no tales, Musgrave deliberately assassinated him upon his own hearth stone. From the peculiarly base character of the assault, the deed sent a wave of horror throughout the land, and a storm of indignation spread far and wide. The assassin was denounced in words of scorn by Sir William Seaton, one of the leading members of the Scottish Commission, and Musgrave was obliged to defend himself by a long and laboured statement of the fray, in which he endeavoured to show that Barngleese was the aggressor, and that he was obliged to kill

M

him 'for', said he, 'my soldiers were in great danger.'

Sir William Seaton writing to Sir Wilfred Lawson gives a very different account of the murder, and characterises the narrative of John Musgrave as 'the slightest purgation he had ever heard in such a case', 'and', says he, 'the country is scandalised at the conduct of John Musgrave and Sir William Hutton'[1], both of whom he accused of dealing in matters of blood. So persistent was Seaton in pressing the charge of deliberate murder against Musgrave, and so absurdly weak was the defence presented by Musgrave and his friends, that the government, after many months of evasions and objections, were compelled to satisfy the public conscience by bringing, or pretending to bring, the assassin to trial. Even the English Commissioners, who had already supped full of horrors and were not easily startled by deeds of blood, found it beyond their power to concoct a decent defence for an atrocity so singularly base. The only one of their number who stood out stoutly in defence of Musgrave was the Lord Bishop of Carlisle, who gave credence to every word of Musgrave's defence, and expressed the opinion that he was amply justified in slaying the old laird as there could be no doubt he and his soldiers were in great danger from Barngleese and his household. The Bishop could see no wrong in the unprovoked assault and robbery in the dead of night. The trial of the murderer was only a sham to satisfy the Scottish Commissioners and did not even interrupt the military duties in which Musgrave was continually employed.

[1] *Muncaster Papers*, Seaton to Lawson, Oct. 4, 1606.

CHAPTER XIX

THE BOGS OF ROSCOMMON

WHILE the sensation caused by the tragic event mentioned in the last chapter was occupying men's minds, evictions were steadily progressing in Eskdale. On June 3rd, 1606, Lawson informs the Council of his operations. 'We have been here', he says, 'since the 20th of May, and shall continue by turns to attend the service. We went thither (to Eskdale) with the Sheriff on the 30th May, and remained until the Earl of Cumberland's officers had taken peaceable possession of divers tenements within his grants, returning the same evening to Carlisle. No resistance was made. We have left to your consideration certain grounds reputed to be part of his Majesty's manor, and not within the forest of Nichol granted to the said Earl. We shall proceed against the Grahams according to your instructions.

'Richard Graham of Randelinton has broken prison. We have reprieved Arthur Graham (of Mote). There is no likelihood of getting a convenient number of them to send away. There are not now remaining in Esk, or within the Earl of Cumberland's grant, much above thirty Grahams, married or unmarried, fit to be sent away to make up the number of those that are returned or dead. Most of those it seems absent themselves, preferring to die at home with shame rather than serve his Majesty abroad with credit'[1].

It will be observed that the clan had the pleasing

[1] *Muncaster Papers*, Commissioners to the Council, June 3, 1606.

option of permanent banishment to the Dutch marches or death on the scaffold, with shame in their native land.

Curiously, this appalling predicament seems to have been thought quite reasonable, and even considerate, in the eyes of King, Council, and Commission.

As for the King, he altogether ignored the possibility that any of the wretched victims under his heel might have their share in those sentiments of love and affection inherent in the human heart. His own gross nature being insensible to such reflections, he stormed on finding that his well-matured plans were being disturbed and delayed by such vexatious obstacles. He hotly resented this clinging to wife and home; this objection to banishment on the part of the Grahams, as the basest ingratitude to himself, considering his great clemency 'in pardoning their lives and in disposing of them, to serve in the garrison towns of Flushing and Brill, places where many honest men desire to be maintained in service.'

James boasted of his clemency in not immediately hanging all the lairds he had ruined without the bother of legal process, for in the opinion of Sir Wilfred Lawson they were all offenders deserving punishment, an opinion which was doubtless shared by the whole race of Musgraves, Taylors, and Fenwicks.

For a considerable time no real progress was made in clearing the country of the condemned clan. The escapes from prison and returns from banishment were more numerous than the arrests. Large numbers were sheltered by relations and former allies on both sides of the Border, and so long as these exasperated individuals were at large there could be little prospect of a comfortable settlement in Eskdale for the Cumberland family.

It was gradually becoming apparent to King and Council that the Carlisle Commission, even when strengthened by the addition of the Lord Bishop, was too weak to carry out the serious task it had undertaken. So closely had the Commissioners devoted their time and attention to the service of Lord Cumberland, and so completely had they ignored the great Border question, for the settlement of which they were called into existence, that reiving and raiding had become as rampant as in the days of Lord Scrope. There was one Scotch nobleman at Court who had considerable experience of the Border, and who was well acquainted with the methods of the outlaws. This was Lord Dunbar, whom the King resolved to send north: not to supersede, but to assist, the Commissioners in wading out of the scandalous enormities and perplexities in which they were struggling. On May 11th, 1606, the Commissioners were advised of the King's intentions in a letter from Dunbar to Lawson, as follows: 'The King at my last parting from his presence, and by letter since the 1st instant, has commanded me to have special care of the Border by the apprehension of the disobedient Grahams, the twenty condemned men who broke Carlisle Castle, and other fugitives and their abettors. I am informed that Sir Richard Lowther of Cumberland gives recett to the Grahams. I pray you to make diligent search in his house about daybreak on the 20th instant, and bring any fugitives you may find there to Carlisle that night, where Sir William Selby will meet you. The good of this service consists in secrecy.' The appointment of Dunbar was also announced in a letter direct from the King's hand. James could not intrust to inferior mortals the handling of questions involving the profounder subtleties of statecraft.

'We do not find', he wrote, 'so good success in your proceedings as we expected. You were ordered to attend directions from our Privy Council from time to time. It seems necessary to ease you of your trouble of sending so far. We have therefore appointed the Earl of Dunbar, who is a councillor in both our kingdoms, and likely to be often at Berwick, to resolve difficulties that may arise in the execution of your service.'

Dunbar was also advised in regard to the scope of his authority by a letter direct from James, in which he says, 'Our meaning is not to give you any authority to proceed as a judge or Commissioner, but to require you to assist the Commissioners with your advice, and we authorize you to cause search to be made for loose persons and to deliver them to the Commissioners.' The duties were to be performed in the saddle rather than in the Council chamber, but whatever limits James intended to impose upon his authority, Dunbar recognised none.

Like the Captain of Bewcastle he smiled at the idea of submission to any higher control than his own will in the perilous campaign among the Border limmers.

Forthwith he assumed the functions of commander-in-chief of the whole Border with supreme power in the sealing of dooms, exactions, and forfeitures, regardless of either James or the lords of the Privy Council.

Being in no way especially interested in the private affairs of Lord Cumberland, he left the remaining Grahams of Eskdale in the hands of Mr. John Musgrave, and advanced along the eastern marches to check the marauders from Liddesdale. His march into Northumberland was crowned with success, many loose persons were captured, but not delivered to the Commissioners as the King had ordered. Dunbar put aside such tedious details as we learn from a letter written by Sir William Seaton to Lawson: 'Dunbar has done good service', he says, ' by executing five men at Foulden who would have "cambered" both countries if they had bene maisters of their heads.'

The great clans of Liddesdale were pursued,

defeated, and scattered. Completely overwhelmed by the greatness of the disaster which had so suddenly overtaken them they were driven back into the hills disheartened, famished, and exhausted. Nearly all the important leaders were captured, and finally Dunbar had the supreme satisfaction of reporting to the Bishop of Carlisle in words carefully attuned to pious ears. 'Man purposeth, and God determyneth', says he, 'Mangerton, Whitehaugh, William Elliot, Andrew Armstrong, and Martin Elliot are executed for very odious and criminal causes, and fourteen others for stealths and other punishable causes.'

Dunbar seems to have known whose heart would be most gladdened by the wholesale character of the butcher's bill. As a matter of course all these men were summarily hanged without trial, or even consultation with the Commissioners, the news of 'the completed job' being all they were allowed to know of the business. It mattered little however to the marauders, as there was no tribunal in England willing to give due consideration to any extenuating fact which might have been urged in their favour. As an example of the disorder and uncertainty in the administration of the law at this period, it is interesting to note that the Bishop of Carlisle and some of his colleagues, after much discussion, found themselves obliged to enquire of the Privy Council what were the proper legal functions of a high sheriff. They had taken fright at the confusion which had gradually arisen between the judicial and the executive duties through the restless activity of Sir Wilfred Lawson, who, though High Sheriff, continued to perform important magisterial duties. 'We wish to know', says the Bishop, 'whether Sir Wilfred Lawson, being High Sheriff, may lawfully sit in judgment in his county. At all the great deliveries, except when Sir Charles Hales (the judge of assize) was here, Sir Wilfred Lawson has given both the charge and the judgment.' He was thus accuser, judge, and executioner all in one, and as by the order of King James, he had full power to arrest, imprison, banish, or hang any one whom he considered 'fit' for such punishments, it is little wonder that even the bishop became alarmed in presence of such stupendous possibilities all gathered into the hands of this very ordinary country gentleman.

It is difficult for us at this day to realize the hideous frequency of capital punishment in the time of King James, when the terror of the scaffold ever stood in the rear of his policy. Trial by jury had degenerated into a farce, and many of the most cherished constitutional rights of the subjects had withered away almost to the point of extinction. The assemblage which still called itself Parliament afforded no protection against the exercise of the most intolerable injustice. Under Elizabeth that institution had become so debased as to fear even to criticize, much less to restrain the murderous excesses of the Crown.

Englishmen thought only of the splendid despotism which had roused their patriotic pride by its great achievements. Strong, alike at home and abroad, Elizabeth had baffled the greatest of all dangers arising from Spanish aggression, and placed her country supreme in the councils of Europe. Dazzled and submissive, they became heedless of their personal liberties, and by gradual, but imperceptible, degrees, they became so apathetic in regard to their essential rights as free-born Britons, that the frequent infliction of capital punishment for offences which were not legally capital according to English law, gave them little or no concern.

Englishmen who have always loved a strong government, were ready to acquiesce in many doubtful deeds for the sake of their great Queen. To this unfortunate state of things the unspeakable King James succeeded, and speedily turned the throne of the mighty Elizabeth into the laughing stock of the world. The great machinery of government headed by Salisbury was, however, ready to his hand, and for many years he was able to revel in the enjoyment of absolute power over the lives and all the material and spiritual interests of his people. So benumbed had the able tyranny of Elizabeth left her subjects, that her miserable successor was enabled to exalt the worthless, to oppress the innocent, to burn old women for impossible crimes, and to shed the blood of his subjects with unconcern for years before unmistakable signs appeared that the people were at last beginning to awake from their degrading lethargy, but more than forty years elapsed before the follies and iniquities of James and his successor were finally trampled in the dust.

It was this extraordinary acquiescence on the part of men completely cowed by long years of tyranny which encouraged a King, so cowardly as James, in that policy of extreme severity which he was always able to explain and defend, in phraseology so lofty and pedantic as to convince the simple people of the profundity of his wisdom. They saw that their King was never in doubt. He had no misgivings as to the soundness of his judgments, and no troublesome modesty ever stood in his way. In the quality of self-satisfaction he had an unchallenged supremacy which bore him along with easy confidence to make known to the world, that he alone among mankind could penetrate and analyse all manner of human dealings with a learned spirit. Judgments which less gifted mortals only reached after patient and laborious investigation, were at once obvious to the great mind of James with little or no help from testimony or argument. His pompous decisions, founded mainly upon conjecture, were given to the world with such a blare of trumpets, and such airs of infallibility, as almost seemed to justify the atrocious penalties with which they were enforced.

It was cause of deep mortification to James to find

that so small a transaction as the destruction of a Border clan in order to establish a domain for his friend and crony Cumberland, had landed his government in a dilemma so hopeless that no solution short of complete extermination of the Grahams seemed possible.

Banishment to the Cautionary towns had proved a complete failure. No plans, however carefully arranged, could hold the Grahams in bondage there, and the monstrosity of punishing their return by death could not be continued indefinitely.

In the midst of his perplexity James received a suggestion from one Sir Ralph Sidley to transport the whole remnant of the Eskdale outcasts to Ireland, where Sidley reckoned that he could, for a consideration, plant them upon certain lands at his disposal in the county of Roscommon. James eagerly accepted this offer, especially as it presented so many advantages which the outcasts would in all probability be so glad to accept that their removal might be accomplished without the exercise of compulsion. Moreover, it was known that several Border Grahams, long settled in the province of Connaught, had prospered exceedingly, and in all likelihood their presence there would be an inducement to their forlorn clansmen to remain as permanent colonists.

On the 24th of June, 1606, came directions from King James to the Commissioners as follows: 'We wish all means to be used for the apprehension of the Grahams who have returned from the Cautionary towns. It appears that divers of the Grahams and other surnames were formerly planted in the province of Connaught, where they have grown to be men of good desert and quality. Sir Ralph Sidley being likely to have the disposing of a great quantity of land called Roscommon, is well able to place forty or fifty families there. He will give you information as to the commodities of the place and the fertility of the ground, which will doubtless be welcome to those who are threatened with the hands of justice. All severity should be laid upon those who are unwilling to go, the greater part of them having deserved punishment.' The last sentence is amusingly characteristic of King James. Believing that a majority of those who refused to go were deserving of death, he thought the easiest, surest, and most equitable remedy was to hang them all, for, at least, they had all been guilty of an unwillingness to remain in Holland. A large number of the younger and more active Grahams were either dead or in hiding when the Irish scheme was projected, and the Commissioners found themselves face to face with starving crowds of the evicted, and certain of the old tenants who had not been removed from their homes. Even Sir Wilfred Lawson seems to have been moved to compassion at sight of the destitute old men, women, and children brought down to abject misery mainly by his zeal and energy in the interest of the Cumberland estates. In a letter addressed by him to Lord Cumberland we not only detect a note of penitence, but an unmistakable insinuation that the deep guilt of the crusade belonged more to his lordship than to him. 'We went', he says, 'with the Sheriff to Arthurett Church, and your officers took possession of divers tenements without resistance. We have reserved the case of Thomas Musgrave of Bewcastle for the consideration of the Council, and also the widow of Brakenhill. We have acquainted some of the principal Grahams with the King's purpose to transport some families to Ireland. We find them so willing that they humbly intreat to be settled in the places appointed before winter. We intend to send the unmarried only within your grants to the Cautionary towns. We pray you to shew compassion towards the wives and children of such as willingly went thither and did not return. We have not favoured the Grahams more than charity bids us.'

The Grahams were now reduced to such a plight that they were willing to go anywhere, so long as they could get beyond the reach of Cumberland's hired bravos, and the merciless Mr. John Musgrave and his horsemen. For months many of them were exposed to cold and hunger; hunted like wild beasts in the woods and among the ruins of their former homes. Old men and women dying of cold under the open sky, and even little children, wearied of their existence, were yielding up their lives with the resignation of old age. These were, however, only vexatious and unavoidable incidents in the execution of his lordship's private business.

A list was forwarded to the Privy Council of those Grahams still in possession of some means dwelling between Esk and Leven. Twenty-three of these were declared to be worth £20 a year. Among them 'Walter Graham of Netherby, his wife and eight children, of whom the eldest is an outlaw, and the second a disorderly person; William Graham of Rose Trees, his wife and six children; Hutchin Graham, alias "young Hutchin", his wife and three children; one Graham at Flushing, and one at Brill.' Forty-three others were described as having less than £20 a year, but all were, in the opinion of the Commissioners, fit for removal to Ireland. Sir Ralph Sidley, the enterprising man of business, had undertaken the settlement of the colony in Roscommon at the moderate rate of £20 for each householder 'wherewith to maintain himself and his family until the land began to yield a profit.' The land was unreclaimed bog, and this slender provision was thought sufficient to provide the means of subsistence during the long and uncertain operations of draining, digging, and improving the soil into crop-bearing condition.

Nearly all the strong young men capable of hard toil had been already swept away, some to the foreign garrisons and many to their graves, so that now, in addition to the old and useless, there was only a moderate sprinkling of middle-aged men who had volunteered for Ireland rather than continue a hopeless struggle in the Eskdale *inferno*. King James, however, seems to have pretended that he believed that this poor, sickly assemblage of outcasts would be able to grapple with the stupendous labours involved in wringing the means of existence from an unreclaimed desert, and the sum of £20 would be an adequate provision for each family while waiting for that distant day when rushes and heather should give place to fields of potatoes and corn.

The Commissioners had, while concentrating the whole of their attention upon the interests of Lord Cumberland, deemed it no part of their duty to think of the ultimate fate of the victims who were driven forth from their homes. It was to them a matter of little moment whether they lived or died so long as they were effectually banished.

A distinct change, however, had taken place since the death of the favourite Earl, upon whom the grant had been conferred, and, though King James was determined to complete the destruction of the clan, it had become with him more a desire for punishing their disobedience than for directly helping the interests of the new Lord Cumberland. In truth the Council was becoming weary of his Lordship's insatiable claims and contentions, the useless arrests and escapes, and the frequent infliction of capital punishment without legal process. The crusade, so far, had been costly, and it was now determined that no more money should flow from the royal treasury for the special benefit of the Cumberland estates. However, as the projected transportation of the Grahams to Ireland was the direct decision of the King, his ministers were obliged to see it carried through. Sir Ralph Sidley had reckoned the cost for transportation and settlement of the families prepared to emigrate at £300, but even this small sum the Council declined to advance.

There was another source, however, from which ministers believed the necessary funds could easily be obtained. They had been misled by Sir Wilfred Lawson and Lord Cumberland into thinking that the northern gentry were eager to make any sacrifice to clear the Border of the Graham clan, whom they 'feared and abhorred.' Labouring under this conviction the Council directed the Commissioners to collect £300 in the shape of voluntary contributions from those terrified gentlemen, and to hand over the amount to Sir Ralph Sidley, who was eagerly awaiting the funds to enable him to carry out his plan of transportations. A period of ominous silence followed the receipt of this order, and in time it began to ooze out that the implacable enemies of the Grahams upon the Border were not so numerous after all. There seemed no burning desire on the part of the inhabitants to see them expelled from the Border, and a distinct objection to subscribe for any such purpose. It became apparent that the Lords of the Council had given a too willing ear to the flood of calumnies pouring in from interested persons on one side until they had come to regard the Grahams as a race almost outside the limits of humanity. Yet, in estimating fairly the worth of the clan in the then state of society, it may be contended that, in point of fidelity, patriotism, and even common honesty, its record was as good as any of the favoured individuals, or families, by whom it was denounced. Every effort was made to exact what the Council was pleased to call a 'voluntary contribution', but neither persuasion, nor even threats, could wring from the people more than about £20, and that small sum was mainly subscribed by four of the most implacable enemies of the Grahams. The Commission had even recourse to the most bare-faced importunity of men while in discharge of their magisterial duties in open Court, where refusal might be injurious to their interests. Not even unfair pressure of this kind had the desired effect. No money came in, on the contrary, the general attitude of sulky refusal seemed directly to negative the charge that the clan was 'feared and abhorred', and might have opened the eyes of a Council of honourable and independent men. After this rebuff the Commissioners' reports became more reserved and less abusive of the clan. With meagre comment they laid the beggarly result of the voluntary offering before the Council as follows: 'List of gentlemen contributors who have promised to pay the following sums towards the transportation of the Grahams: Christopher Pickering, Sheriff of Cumberland, £5; Sir Edward Musgrave, £5; Sir William Hutton, £4; Sir John Dalston refused on the Bench in open Court; Thomas Salkeld, £2; Henry Dacre, £2 10s.; Richard Curwen, £2; Richard Dalton, £2; and twenty-eight others offer sums varying from 20 shillings to 2s. 6d. Thomas Thompson, Gent., John Lancaster, Gent., and William Cowx refused to contribute'[1].

The King was surprised and indignant on receiving these wretched contributions in aid of his meritorious campaign. He severely censured the northern gentry on their backwardness in offering their money, especially Sir John Dalston, and demanded a list of all those men of means who had failed to subscribe. The effect of this was that Sir John Dalston and many of his neighbours found it their wisest policy to pay up; though, even with this method of coercion there was no adequate result. The attempt had only proved that in spite of ancient feuds and animosities there were singularly few living upon the Border who desired the destruction of what had formerly been the greatest of all the clans. As the people declined to subscribe, James

[1] *Muncaster MSS.*, f. 132, Commissioners to Salisbury, July 30, 1606.

determined to compel them. He ordered a rate to be levied upon the surrounding district; ostensibly, of course, to clear the country of malefactors, but, in reality, it was a tax upon the people for the benefit of Lord Cumberland's estates. Curiously it does not seem to have occurred to the King or his ministers that the nobleman who had received a free gift of all the fertile lands of lower Eskdale might have, himself, discharged these last expenses from his own resources. The people were expelled in his interest, and yet he could meanly see his neighbours rated to pay for the last mournful flitting of those who had been ruined and cast out of their homes by the decree of a crazy King for the enrichment of himself and his family.

The rate having been imposed, the £300 was collected and passed into the hands of Sir Ralph Sidley. With what scrupulous fidelity he performed his task we shall presently see.

CHAPTER XX

FINAL PACIFICATION OF THE BORDER

WHEN arrangements had been completed the pitiful crowd of old and young, uprooted from their Eskdale homes, were soon on their way stumbling hopelessly along towards Workington, the port of embarkation, under military guard. On September 13th, 1606, the Commissioners report to Lord Salisbury, ' We have sent the chief Grahams to the port of Workington under the conduct of the Sheriff of Cumberland, with the assistance of the County and of Mr. John Musgrave's horsemen. We have not been able to send away fifty families, because some of the poorer sort who had yielded themselves into transportation, at the instant thereof fled, out of weariness of their bondage to their masters, the chief Grahams. There are not now left between Leven and Sark more than three Grahams of ability, of whom two are more than eighty years of age. All the notorious offenders, whose manner terrified peaceable people, are gone away. Some of their wives who cannot go now will follow in the spring. By their clamours and our entreaties, they have been allowed to gain the corn, hay, and grass of this season without any allowance of rent to the Earl of Cumberland, so that he will have little profit of his signiorie this year. We find Sir Ralph Sidley well affected to use the Grahams well if they shall so deserve. We have committed to him the £300 levied from the county.

' Although Esk, Sark, and Leven are purged of evil men, their remain others fit to follow in Bewcastle and Gillisland. The Grahams carry with them many horses and household stuffs. There are yet remaining outlaws the sons of Walter Graham of Netherby and divers others'[1].

The arrangement with Sidley was so vague, and his responsibilities so ill defined as to lead him to suppose that he was invested with full discretionary power to deal with the funds entrusted to him in accordance with his own humour or his own caprice. He was under no contract more binding for the care and relief of the outcasts than the mild advice of the Commissioners 'to use the Grahams well if they so deserved', and there was nothing in the arrangement to prevent Sir Ralph from appropriating the whole of the funds to his own use, and leaving the emigrants to perish. Taking advantage of this loose understanding, he paid little attention to his charge after their embarkation; apparently unable to discover in any one of the assemblage that standard of desert entitling him to pecuniary help. Consequently, thinking his services not much needed, he pocketed the funds and decamped. All his fine promises as to the needful provision of food and shelter for the families on their arrival upon his lands in Roscommon proved to be moonshine, for he was simply one of those titled rascals swarming in England during the reign of King James. There is on record an appeal from the emigrants signed by William Graham of Medopp, and others, depicting the woeful plight in which the banished people found themselves on reaching their destination. They say that the little money they had amongst them was all spent and they had nothing wherewith to get food. Some of them had travelled a day's journey in search of Sir Ralph Sidley, but without success, and but for the succour they received from two knights of their name and race who met them on their arrival, 'and comforted

[1] *Muncaster MSS*, f. 142, Commissioners to Salisbury, Sept. 13, 1606.

them with kindly entertainment and promises of help', their fate must have been as appalling as that of their kindred on the Dutch sands. The Council thought its duty complete by merely requesting the Lord Deputy of Ireland to moderate any differences that might arise between the Grahams to be transported and their landlord Sir Ralph Sidley, 'For', say they, 'the Counties of Cumberland and Westmorland having sustained great losses from the Grahams, have contributed a great sum of money to redeem their peace.'

The condition of the outcasts having become wholly desperate, many of them fled rather than face starvation, and, by some means found their way home to the Border to the surprise and vexation of the authorities. The wrath of the King, on hearing that several of them had returned from their costly and 'comfortable' settlement in Roscommon, can be more easily imagined than described. The King, in his wisdom, as usual, knew all the facts of the situation as it were, by intuition or some process of deduction too profound for ordinary minds, and there was no necessity for him to ascertain the exact facts as to how it came to pass that men who a month ago, had willingly and thankfully agreed to transportation into Ireland should so speedily have changed their minds, and returned to Eskdale at the risk of their lives. It was enough for the King that they had committed the unpardonable offence of disobedience, and had wounded his feelings by their ingratitude in the face of his munificent clemency in sparing their lives. His Majesty was always impatient of details which were wearisome and unnecessary when he had made up his mind; and so, knowing literally nothing of the ghastly wilderness into which the outcasts had been lured by the perfidy of Sir Ralph Sidley, he sent his well-considered judgment of the case through his Council, to the despairing Sir Wilfred Lawson and his colleagues sitting at Carlisle. 'The Grahams who have returned from Ireland', he writes, 'deserve the least favour. You are to proceed against them in justice (hanging) both for their offences and for the sake of example to others. Those who have returned from the cautionary towns, and those fugitives who voluntarily enter themselves may have the favour of transportation to Ireland if they give good security for their speedy departure thither. Let justice proceed against those who cannot give good caution for their departure and those who are still fugitives. We have written to the Lord Deputy of Ireland desiring him to deal earnestly with Sir Ralph Sidley for such good usage of the Grahams as may encourage them to continue there'[1].

James seemed all unconscious of the irony of his words, convinced of his generosity in extending the favour of transportation to men whose lives were at his mercy, and to whom, in his goodness, he had left the choice between the desolate bogs in Ireland and the scaffold at home; he now agreed to re-transportation on the condition that they could find security for their departure by a certain date, failing which they were to be consigned to the gallows as an example to others. A few more capital punishments practically brought the struggle to an end. Many of the banished clan found new homes in various parts of Ireland where they prospered, and many returned to the Border, where, in happier times, they settled again into their old haunts, becoming excellent members of society.

As the sensations in Eskdale gradually subsided, interest was transferred to the campaign in Liddesdale and on the Northumbrian border, where the forces under Lord Durham were in active operation. And although we find him assuring the Bishop of Carlisle that the jails of Berwick and

[1] *Muncaster MSS.*, f. 165, Council to Commissioners, Dec. 24, 1606.

Newcastle were full of felons and malefactors, no real impression had as yet been made upon the rooted evil of Border raiding. The execution of popular leaders only aggravated the disorder by bringing a greater and greater number of angry relatives and friends into the field, adding to the ranks of the reivers many of those who had taken to pursuits of peace. The more relentless the warfare, the more determined became the resistance and wider grew the area of disturbance. Carlisle jail became so crowded that the Bishop was obliged to summon Sir Wilfred from his home at Isell to consult with him regarding the seriously pestered condition of the prison, which was daily growing worse. He expresses the hope that the jail delivery which is approaching will considerably reduce the inmates by the free application of the rope, and so prevent the spread of the disease. The Bishop, true to his county, says to Lawson, 'Come sufficiently well armed to answer all Scotch objections (at the meeting of the joint Commission) like a right Cumberland man. A precise account will be required of what justice has been done on both sides. Expect to bear the whole burden yourself of what has been done on the English side.'

So far as the English Commission was concerned, it had proved a despicable failure, for, with the exception of the destruction of the Grahams, it had done nothing but embitter the hatred existing between the two countries. Not a single step had been taken in the delicate and important work of smoothing down international and family animosities. The demand of the Scotch Commissioners for 'an enrolment of all the feuds between the two countries, so that all parties interested in matters of blood unreconciled should appear and give in their griefs' had met with no response.

To the Borderer of those days his feud was part of his life, as essential to his existence as are their grievances to the Irish patriots of our own day. To ask him to divest his mind of the great family hatred instilled into him with his mother's milk, the deadly feud of his forefathers which must in turn pass to his sons, and which lay at the root of all that was sensational and daring in his life, was to ask the impossible. For the solution of the Border problem a more hopeful remedy soon came in view than the Commission of local magnates, this was the employment of the one man within the kingdom who thoroughly understood the Border game, and who had personal knowledge of nearly all the fraternity by whom the game was played. This was the great prince of raiders of bygone days—the bold Buccleuch—the direct descendant of that famous Scott of Buccleuch by whom the clans were originally organised into formidable raiding bands.

Buccleuch had had a charmed life, and considering his numerous invasions of England it is marvellous how he escaped the rope. He, alone, among the great chieftains had exercised a far-seeing and wise discretion, even in his wild career, which ultimately bore him along, through all risks, threats and reproaches, to the dignity of a peerage and a seat in the councils of his King.

> Then up and spake the noble King,
> And an angry man I vow was he,
> 'It ill becomes ye, bauld Buccleuch,
> To talk o' rief or felonie,
> For if every man had his ain cow
> A richt puir clan your name would be.'

But Scott was now earnestly enlisted on the side of law and order and enthusiastically anxious for the success of the Union. He had already utilised his knowledge of Border tenacity and courage by raising a troop of 200 from various clans for the campaign in the Low Countries. Under his command these clansmen rendered splendid service, but few of them ever returned to tell the tale. The arrival of

Buccleuch from the Belgic wars, where he had gained distinction, at the moment when Border affairs were at their worst, was peculiarly opportune, as he alone was the great physician who could diagnose the disease and had the skill and courage to cut deep into its roots. King James and his Council, therefore, gladly availed themselves of the potent service of this great past-master in all those arts and wiles in the Border game of plunder which had been the chief occupation of the house of Buccleuch for ages, and which, by a strange decree of fate, he, the most notorious of all his race, became the chosen instrument for its final suppression. How ample were the powers with which he was invested the following remarkable documents will show.

The King writes as follows: 'There occurred to our memory our most dear cousin Walter, Lord Scott of Buccleuch, a man of energy, prompt in council and action, powerful in fortune, force, arms and following, to whom we found and esteemed that enterprise worthy to be entrusted on account of his past famous and honourable services done to us and the Commonwealth, and on account of his great fidelity in times by past in executing with honour and dignity the affairs we entrusted to him, and that to the great help and welfare of our loyal, dutiful and obedient subjects, and in punishing malefactors and refractory and rebellious persons.'

Buccleuch's great final raid proved the death-blow to the last of the important limmers. Every leading Outlaw was hunted down and slain without mercy, while an order was issued for the demolition of all peels and strongholds along the Border, save only the dwellings of the Nobles and Barons, and thus the first distinct step was taken to cure the Border evil. Buccleuch has been blamed, and with some reason, for his merciless treatment of old allies, many of whom were trained and matured under his own wing, and his scant consideration for the helpless women and children whose evil fate had fixed their dwellings in that stormy country.

The time had come, however, when nothing but the most drastic remedy could o'ermaster the chronic disease of ages, and though, doubtless, many innocent persons perished in the conflict with the marauders, it may be, in some degree, excused as the unavoidable price which the world has often been compelled to pay in the interest of its advancing civilization.

Some curious details of the Buccleuch campaign, may be quoted:

'His Majesty had entrusted him', we are told, 'both privately and in public, that he should, with the utmost speed and expedition, take measures to execute justice on the malefactors, and settle the country in peace. In the execution of these commands the Lord Buccleuch was necessitated to use fire-raising, to cast down, demolish, and destroy castles, houses, and buildings, to use hostile feud in hostile manner against the malefactors, as well in taking their lives, in killing and slaying of them, as in putting them to exile and banishing them from the bounds. In consequence of the lack of prisons, and to prevent the importunate intercession of certain good persons, the most part of these desperate men at once, and immediately on their apprehension, were necessarily hanged and punished with death by pit and gallows off-hand, on the spot at which they were apprehended, dispensing with the ordinary forms of justice as they were publicly known, and without any dread and with the utmost audacity confessed and openly acknowledged these, and many others, capital crimes and enormities, as if they should not have been prevented from perpetrating them, also in executing the King's directions and commands in slaying and killing the fugitives and others resisting by force of arms against being taken and presented to justice and doom. His Majesty declares that the Lord Buccleuch had acted well, dutifully and honourably, and the furthering and establishing of the peace and the quietness of his kingdom. Lord Scott was therefore absolved and free from all questionings and charges which might be moved against these causes. He was therefore exonerated from all pains, charges, and peril which might be imputed to him.'

Although the forces of disorder were broken and all the clans dissolved and scattered by the drastic measures of Buccleuch, it required more than a hundred years before the old grudges and jealousies between the two countries died down sufficiently to permit of cordial and advantageous intercourse. In time, however, by the influence of the church, the introduction of the parochial system of education, and the impartial administration of the law, the old raiding habits were given up in favour of honest industry, and the district once so famous, or so infamous, as the scene of the notorious deeds of the 'ill week' may now be described as one of the most peaceful and law-abiding parts of the kingdom.

Many of the Scotts, Kers, Elliots, Grahams, and other descendants of the raiders have, in modern times, brought to bear their inherited force of character on the social, intellectual, and scientific life of their country, and the keen appreciation of ancient Border chivalry by the native poets, notably Scott and Hogg, has been the means of throwing an air of undying romance over the doughty deeds of the great clansmen of former days, a stirring example of which is Hogg's *Lariston* :

> Lock the door, Lariston, lion of Liddesdale;
> Lock the door, Lariston, Lowther comes on ;
>   The Armstrongs are flying,
>   The widows are crying,
> The Castleton's burning and Oliver's gone !
>
> Lock the door, Lariston,—high on the weather-gleam
> See how the Saxon plumes bob on the sky—

Yeoman and carbinier,
Bilman and halberdier,
Fierce is the foray, and far is the cry.

Bewcastle brandishes high his proud scimitar;
Ridley is riding his fleet-footed grey !
Hidley and Howard there,
Wandale and Windermere ;
Lock the door, Lariston ; hold them at bay.

Why dost thou smile, noble Elliot of Lariston ?
Why does the joy-candle gleam in thine eye ?
Thou bold Border ranger,
Beware of thy danger ;
Thy foes are relentless, determined, and nigh.

I have Mangerton, Ogilvie, Raeburn, and Netherbie,
Old Sim of Whitram and all his array ;
Come all Northumberland,
Teesdale and Cumberland,
Here at the Breaken tower end shall the fray !

Shrill was the bugle's note ! dreadful the warrior's shout !
Lances and halberts in splinters were borne ;
Helmet and hauberk then
Braved the claymore in vain,
Buckler and armlet in shivers were shorn.

Lightning Source UK Ltd.
Milton Keynes UK
UKHW021940250619
345040UK00005B/42/P